A Beginner's Guide to the Chakra System
Unravelling the Mystery

Brenda Hunt

Copyright © Brenda Hunt 2013
All rights reserved world wide
No part of 'A Beginner's Guide to the Chakra System' may be reproduced or stored by any means without the express permission of Brenda Hunt

Whilst reasonable care is taken to ensure the accuracy of the information in this publication, no responsibility can be accepted for the consequences of any actions based on any opinions, information or advice found in the publication.

Healing information contained in this publication should not be taken as a substitute for professional medical advice. You should always consult your doctor on serious matters.

ISBN-13: 978-1484973066
ISBN-10: 1484973062

Contents

Introduction 7
The Chakras 10
   The kundalini 15
Chakra System and influences 18
The seven major chakras 20
The Root Chakra (1st) 20
The Sacral Chakra (2nd) 24
The Solar Plexus Chakra (3rd) 27
The Heart Chakra (4th) 30
The Throat Chakra (5th) 33
The Third Eye Chakra (6th) 36
The Crown Chakra (7th) 39
Other chakras 42
   The Minor Chakras 42
      The foot chakras 43
      The knee chakras 43
      The gonad chakras 44
      The spleen chakra 44
      The stomach chakra 44
      The liver chakra 45
      The hand chakras 45
      The breast chakras 46
      The clavicle chakras 47
      The eye chakras 47

The temple chakras 47
The thymus chakra....................................... 47
The transpersonal chakras.................................. 48
The 4th Eye Chakra 48
The 5th Eye Chakra 48
The Earth Star Chakra............................... 48
The Soul Star Chakra 49

Hormones and the 7 Major Chakras 50
What exactly are Hormones?..................................... 50
The root chakra – Ovaries/testes............................ 51
The sacral chakra –Adrenal glands......................... 52
The solar plexus chakra – Pancreas......................... 53
The heart chakra – thymus..................................... 54
The throat chakra – thyroid.................................... 55
The third eye chakra – Pituitary 56
The crown chakra – Pineal 57

Crystal healing and the Chakra System..59
The Root Chakra 60
The Sacral Chakra 62
The Solar Plexus Chakra............................... 62
The Heart Chakra 63
The Throat Chakra... 64
The Third Eye Chakra.................................... 65
The Crown Chakra... 65
Cleansing your crystals 66
Programming clear quartz....................................... 70
Crystal Healing Layouts... 71
Basic Chakra layout 71
The Seal of Solomon..................................... 73
Chakra realignment....................................... 75
Other ways of using the Chakra points........ 76

Dowsing and The Chakra System 77
- Programming your pendulum. 78
- Dowsing the Chakra system 80
- Dowsing to balance your own chakras 82

Aromatherapy and the chakra system. ... 84
- The root chakra. 86
- The sacral chakra. 87
- The solar plexus chakra. 87
- The heart chakra 88
- The throat chakra. 88
- The third eye chakra 88
- The crown chakra 89
- Working with essential oils. 90
  - Chakra massage 91
  - Aromatherapy bath. 92
  - Aromatherapy hair oil. 93
  - Steam inhalation. 93
  - Vaporisation. 93

Colour healing and the chakras 95
- The root chakra 96
- The sacral chakra 97
- The solar plexus chakra 97
- The heart chakra 97
- The throat chakra 97
- The third eye chakra 98
- The Crown chakra 98

Healing from within 99
- The root chakra 100
- The sacral chakra 101
- The solar plexus chakra 102
- The heart chakra 102

- The throat chakra.. 103
- The third eye chakra.................................. 104
- The crown chakra 104

Working with the chakra system. 106
- The root chakra.. 107
- The sacral chakra... 112
- The solar plexus chakra............................. 117
- The heart chakra.. 120
- The throat chakra.. 124
- The Third Eye Chakra.................................. 129
- The Crown chakra. 134

And into the future 137
About the Author 138

Introduction

You will come across the word chakra in many different areas of study - crystal healing, Reiki, yoga, colour healing, sound therapy and many other energy-based therapies.

But what are chakras?

So many of the books that you read and so much of the information that is available, seem to assume that you already know what the chakras are, what they do for you, how to work with them, how they affect you and how you can affect them. But where do you start?

Well, hopefully – here! I've written this book as your guide to the chakra system.

How do you work with the Chakras?

How do they affect everyday life?

And how can you help keep your system in balance with different techniques and how can you improve your health when you know about the Chakras?

Understanding the Chakra system can help you bring balance to all areas of your life - emotional, mental, physical and spiritual.

And understanding how each Chakra can affect different parts of your body and your life can help bring problems into focus, letting you see how physical problems can be linked to emotional stresses and mental worries.

The Chakra System is a 'system' and I believe it should be treated as a whole, complete system rather than focusing on a single chakra at a time.

In the West, we are so used to seeing our bodies as a collection of parts - a broken leg, high cholesterol, asthma, a bad heart, a serious infection - that we seem to have forgotten that we are a whole person and should be treated as a whole person, and the same is true of chakra healing.

We have developed a tendency to focus on a single chakra, such as the root chakra or the heart chakra. But treating the chakras as individuals can create imbalance in the entire system. In the same way that taking a medicine to solve one problem can cause other problems because of the side effects of the drug, treating one chakra extensively can cause problems in the energy flow throughout the entire system and leads to other unintentional problems.

That is why I have broken this book down into various sections about the effects the chakra system can have on you, and how you work on them. Rather than deal with each chakra at a time, with all the different healing methods and everything about it in individual sections for each chakra, starting at the root chakra and working to the crown chakra, I have dealt with the major chakra system - that is the seven chakras in line with the spine - from different healing points of view and methods.

So, if you are interested in crystal healing you can go to the section on crystal healing. If you are interested in the endocrine system you can jump to the section on chakras and the hormones, or if you want a bit more information about how each chakra can actually affect you, you can skip the rest and go straight there!

Of course I'd love you to read the whole book from beginning to end, absorbing all of my words as you go – but it's okay – feel free to dip in and out as you want!

Understanding the chakras, how they affect you, how your energy flows through them, how you can improve your health and your well-being through understanding and balancing the chakras, is a fascinating journey.

But you don't have to be an advanced practitioner, a specially gifted healer, a deeply spiritual guide or a master of mystic knowledge to be able to understand and translate the mysteries of the chakras. I hope that by the end of this book - or skipping in and out of it as you prefer - you will have a much clearer understanding of how you can work with your chakra system to improve everyday life, your physical health, emotional well being, bringing you a sense of peace and calm mentally and spiritually.

The Chakras

So what are the chakras?

Ancient Indian Sanskrit texts teach us of the Chakra system. They tell of centres of energy in the human body, with seven major points arranged along the line of the spine.

The word Chakra means 'wheel' or 'disk', which is a good description. They are generally seen as a vortex, a spiritual whirlpool, where metaphysical energy enters your own energy field. Each chakra is positioned at a major centre of the body, coinciding with the endocrine system.

Our modern Western medicine can and regularly does produce incredible treatments, but it does tend to see us as a biological machine, a collection of parts which can be fixed, suppressed, removed, and even replaced. This is wonderful if you have a serious infection that can be killed with antibiotics or if your arteries are beginning to block up and can be reopened with a stent.

People have their lives not only saved but transformed by some of the advanced treatments available to us. But there are bad sides as well as good.

Many medicines have an incredible list of side effects. Some actually cause other diseases and then require other medicines to fix those problems. Some people end up with a cupboard full of different potions and pills and often they don't even know what each one is supposed to be doing.

We expect our modern medical treatment to be quick and the results to be immediate, allowing us to go back to work within days, even after major surgery, rather than taking time to rest and recover.

We seem to have developed a habit of seeing time resting as time wasted, a weakness, even a sign of laziness. We have become disconnected from the nature of our own system and no longer listen to the messages our bodies is trying desperately to send.

Eastern systems of energy healing look at the body in a totally different way.

It sees us as a 'whole'.

Not only a complete physical body, where each part interacts with the rest, but as a complete energy body, where physical illness can be linked to emotional stress, spiritual distress or mental stress.

As we become more aware of this in the West, we have become more aware of energy healing and chakra healing.

The chakras balance and control the flow of subtle energies in the body. This subtle energy system affects the physical, mental, emotional and spiritual energy that makes up our whole system and when we take a holistic view of healing, we can see that physical illness often has its source in the other areas of our energy field.

Our modern lifestyle is not kind to our overall holistic well-being. We talk about the 24/7 society and we often try to live 24/7. We work long hours, travel long distances, commute for hours, take work home and work weekends. Worse still, with the latest technology of smartphones and tablets, many people are checking their work emails at all times of the day and night, even in bed! It's certainly not 9-5 anymore.

And then, when we're not working, we expect to be out shopping or at restaurants and bars, meeting friends, taking part in sports or partying. Even when we're supposed to be resting on holiday we often fly to the other side of the world, spend our time partying and rushing around seeing the sights and then fly back.

And then there's multitasking. It's not enough to be working flat on at one just thing, you have to be on facebook, or blogging and tweeting about it at the same time!

Needing to sleep eight hours a night is seen as a weakness, when in fact, sleep is our recovery time. It's a time when our body repairs itself, when our brain processes the information it has gathered during the day and prepares us for the next day.

Good quality sleep, and enough of it, is part of keeping us healthy.

It's no wonder that during our hectic, modern daily life, our chakras can become unbalanced.

When the energy flow does become unbalanced, speeds up or becomes blocked, this can hinder the flow of energy throughout the body.

Over time this can contribute to physical illness, serious stress or emotional upset. Even seemingly fit people with active lifestyles can suddenly succumb to a serious illness such as a stroke or heart attack. Chronic fatigue syndrome (M.E.) tends to hit people who have been extremely active, both mentally and physically, with the kind of appointment diary that would make most people tired just to read it!

We are very complex systems, and many illnesses cannot be treated simply, even though we'd like to think that they could be nowadays. All parts of our body interact with each other and we should treat ourselves as a whole rather than as a collection of parts.

Keeping our energy system in balance is a vital part of maintaining our general well-being and the chakra system is the route for keeping this energy flowing.

In Eastern Yogic texts, the chakras are visualised as lotus flowers, with the petals and fine roots of the flower distributing the life force – or

Prana – throughout the physical body and converting the energy into chemical, hormonal and cellular changes.

As we've seen, there are seven major chakras in line with the spine, which follow the endocrine system of our physical bodies.

The number seven corresponds to many things in nature.

There are seven colours in the rainbow, the different wavelengths of light that are shown when pure white light is diffracted when it is disbursed through a prism or the water droplets in rain.

There are seven days in the week, seven notes on a musical scale. The world has seven continents and the pH balance for pure water is seven.

The number seven was considered sacred in antiquity. The Egyptians had seven original and higher gods. There were Seven Wonders of the World, followers of Mithra the Persian God, had a complex system with seven grades of initiation into the mystical religion.

There are many more examples of the importance of the number seven in nature, in religion and in ancient civilisations. Seven is a universally important number, so it is no surprise that there are seven major chakras in the human body.

The chakras are not physically visible in the body, even though they are closely associated with the endocrine system, so you can't actually see them, although you can feel the energy moving through them, especially if there is a sudden flow of energy through one of the chakras in something like a Reiki treatment.

The vibration of crystals can harmonise the Chakras and allow the energy to flow freely again, which is why it can be helpful to use a chakra healing layout with a number of different gemstones as well as the more direct use of a crystal or crystals that are specifically linked to the problem or illness that you want to treat.

Different crystals are different colours, and the vibrational energy of the colours is linked to each chakra and for this type of healing, the colour is an important part of the choice that you make. There is more information on working with healing crystals and the chakras in a later chapter.

You can also work with dowsing, aromatherapy, colour, herbal medicine and foods to help keep your system in balance.

The kundalini

In reading about the chakras, you will often come across reference to the kundalini and awakening the kundaline, referring to this mysterious thing as if you should automatically know what they're talking about.

So what is it?

The kundalini is the mythical serpent that sleeps coiled three and a half times at the base of the spine, at the Root Chakra, blocking the rise of energy - also referred to as the life force, prana or chi - from the earth though your chakra system.

It represents the life force that rises up through the chakra system, changing your energy field, and therefore your life on all levels. Balancing the root chakra allows the kundalini to awaken and begin the release of its energy through your system.

Although there is a great deal written about awakening the kundalini, treating it sometimes as if this is the only purpose of working with your chakra system, it is actually a very powerful force and should not be treated lightly.

In the teachings of Yoga, there are two nerve currents in the spinal column, called Pingala on the right which contains ascending vitality, and Ida on the left, containing descending vitality, and a hollow canal called Sushumna running through the spinal-cord.

These Nadis or streams are the subtle channels through which the life force or prana circulates.

At the lower end of the hollow canal is what the Yogis call the 'lotus of the kundalini' where the kundalini sleeps coiled up. When that kundalini awakes it tries to force the passage through this hollow canal, and as it rises, step-by-step, layer after layer of the mind becomes open. When it reaches the crown chakra, the Yogi is perfectly detached from the body, and the mind and soul finds itself free.

The kundalini image of the life force being represented by a snake is seen throughout history, and throughout religions. In fact, even today, the medical profession uses the symbol of the caduceus with the two snakes or serpents entwined around the staff of healing.

A Beginners Guide

Chakra System and influences

Although the rest of this book will go into much more detail about the areas of influence for each chakra, this is a quick and simple overall guide for the seven major chakras.

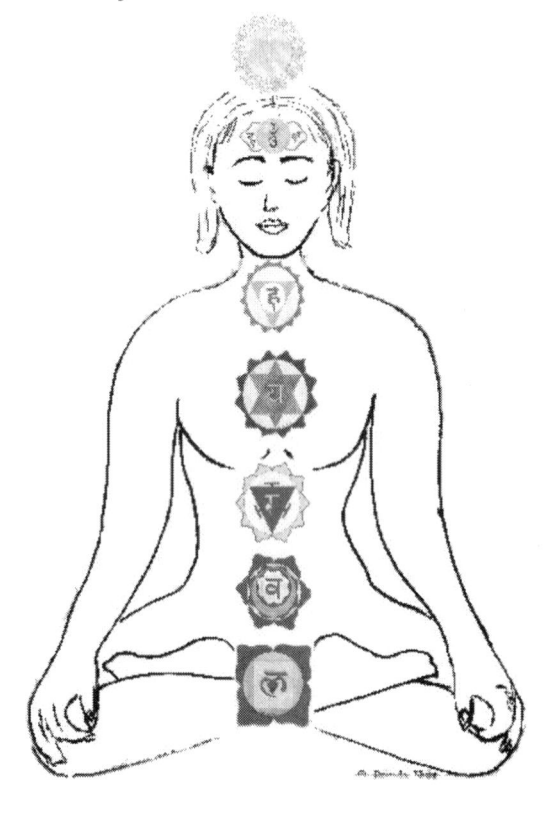

Root Reproductive - stability, adrenal glands, survival, trust, ego, practicality, confidence, energy distribution

Sacral Genito-urinary - sexuality, fertility, reproductive, intuition, feelings, creativity

Solar plexus Digestive - stomach, pancreas, emotions, stress, self confidence

Heart Circulatory - blood pressure, immune system, love, compassion, healing, personal growth

Throat Respiratory - hearing, lymphatic system, communication, creativity, personal expression

Third eye Autonomic nervous - pituitary, eyes, mental and emotional balance, understanding, mental organisation

Crown Central nervous system - mental clarity, consciousness, perception, nerves, sleep, intuition, inspiration.

The seven major chakras

Although there are other chakras in the body – in the feet, in the hands – and others surrounding the body – the earth star, the soul star – most areas of chakra balancing and healing concentrate on the seven major chakras that are in line with the spine, from the base of the spine, where we sit, to the crown at the very top of our head and it is these chakras that we will be focusing on – so what are they?

The Root Chakra (1st)

Maladhara – Mal = root

Adhara = support, vital part

Also known as the earth chakra the 'root of our support'

Located at the base of the spine, situated where your body meets the earth when you sit.

This is the chakra that controls our ability to be grounded. It is associated with physical energy and physical health. If this is blocked you can feel anxious, insecure, frustrated.

Physically it can cover osteoarthritis, obesity, problems with the feet and legs, haemorrhoids and constipation and chronic long term illnesses.

Colours: Red, black, dark brown

Crystals: red Jasper, red tiger's eye, ruby, garnet, hematite, pietersite, smoky quartz, black tourmaline, black onyx, obsidian

- Gland: Adrenal
- Sense: Smell
- Colour: Red, dark brown or black
- Intake: Protein
- Element: Earth
- Oils: Patchouli, cedarwood, myrrh, lavender, frankincense
- Symbol: 4 crimson petal lotus flower, around a yellow square containing a downward pointing triangle
- Masculine – Yang

Areas of effect

This is the chakra that controls our ability to be grounded. In fact, the nerve bundle at this chakra resembles a massive root system. It leaves the spine and runs down both legs as the sciatic nerve, to the heels and the tip of your toes.

It is associated with physical energy and physical health. Survival, being grounded, health, vitality and fitness. It is the chakra for the spinal column, the feet and legs, large intestine and kidneys and of course, the sciatic nerve.

Balance

When the root chakra is balanced you are grounded. You feel a sense of security and stability, a feeling of 'being at home', both with yourself and your past, it gives you a trust in the natural order of things. You have energy and good general health

It is very important to have this chakra balanced. There is a tendency to concentrate on the higher, more spiritual, more glamorous chakras at the expense of the root, sacral and solar plexus chakras, but it's very important to remember that we are 'whole' beings and therefore need to keep the 'whole' system in balance.

The root chakra is directly linked to the crown chakra and is the foundation of your entire energy system. It is the chakra that gives you a solid base in reality and keeps you grounded as well as being vital for physical energy and general good health.

Imbalance

When there is imbalance in this chakra, it can manifest in problems with food – either obesity or being underweight - greed in food and in general. You can feel anxious, insecure, frustrated. It can cover osteoarthritis, problems with the feet and legs, haemorrhoids and constipation, problems with the bones and teeth.

It can also cause low energy problems or chronic fatigue or mental lethargy as well as an inability to find inner stillness or peace. Imbalance can also cause excess worry about security or money fears, leading you to crave security and rigid rules and boundaries to an almost addictive degree.

You have to pay special attention to the base chakra in any case of chronic ill-health – for instance M.E./CFS – or in cases of lack of security. It is literally your base and whatever else you want to achieve, you must be strong physically.

The Sacral Chakra (2nd)

Svadhisthana – Sva = vital force : adhisthana = seat or abode

Also known as the water chakra or sweetness - 'In your own dwelling place'

Located 1" below the navel. and above the genitals.

This balances sexuality, emotion, desire, creativity, intuition and self worth. If it is blocked you may feel emotionally explosive, lacking energy, have feelings of isolation. Physically it can lead to kidney and uterine disorders, lower back pain, impotence and prostate problems

Crystals: carnelian, orange calcite, aragonite, amber, orange sapphire

- Gland: ovaries/testes
- Sense: taste
- Colour: orange
- Intake: fluids
- Element: water
- Oils: rose, jasmine, sandalwood, ginger, ylang ylang, orange
- Symbol: 6 petal orange-red lotus flower containing 2nd lotus flower and an upward pointing crescent moon
- Feminine - Yin

Areas of effect

This chakra is connected with sexual energy, affecting attraction, emotion, vitality, desire, creativity, intuition, self worth, sexuality, the reproductive system and all fluid functions of the body- that is, the bladder and kidneys, prostate, lymphatic system, fat deposits and skin.

Balanced

The sacral chakra is a spiritual centre. When it is balanced and activated you will have vitality and health will flow. You have good self esteem, a sense of direction, emotional stability and a healthy relationship to desire, pleasure and intimacy.

You are able to trust and be expressive, you are attuned to your feelings and emotions and are able to see the positive side of situations.

The balance of the sacral chakra allows you to find pleasure in life, approaching things with enthusiasm, being willing to enjoy life and concentrate on the positive aspects of existence.

People with a balanced sacral chakra are often seen as 'lucky', but it is just that they tend to see the good in situations rather than the negatives

Imbalance

Imbalance can manifest as impotence, frigidity or an addiction to sex, emotional immaturity, a tendency to jealousy, fear of intimacy, guilt and obsession. You may feel emotionally explosive, lacking energy or have feelings of isolation.

Physically it can lead to kidney and uterine disorders, IBS, lower or middle back pain, impotence and prostate problems, infertility.

The Solar Plexus Chakra (3rd)

Manipuraka – manas = mind : surya = sun

Also known as the power chakra. 'dwelling place of jewels'.

Located below the breastbone and behind the stomach. From the back of the body, it is just below the shoulder blades.

It is also known as the power chakra and is associated with personal power, ambition, anger and joy, intellectual activity and the central nervous system. If this chakra is blocked you can lack confidence, worry about the opinions of others, be oversensitive to criticism, suffer low self esteem or have an addictive personality.

Physically it can cover digestive problems, stomach ulcers, diabetes, chronic fatigue and allergies.

Crystals: citrine, yellow sapphire, golden tiger's eye, yellow jasper, topaz

- Gland: pancreas
- Sense: sight
- Colour: yellow
- Intake: starch
- Element: fire

- Oils: vetiver, cinnamon, geranium, lemon grass, peppermint
- Symbol: 10 petal yellow lotus flower containing a deep red, down pointing triangle
- Masculine - Yang

Areas of effect

The solar plexus chakra is associated with personal power, ambition, anger and hatred, joy and laughter, intellectual activity, logic. The muscles, pancreas and adrenals, stomach, digestive system, gall bladder, liver, spleen and the central nervous system.

Balanced

When it is balanced you have a strong sense of identity and no need to overpower others in order to feed a sense of self. It brings vitality, spontaneity and a positive will power.

You are optimistic, tolerant, able to adapt to situations and be flexible, tending to follow your gut reactions and respond instinctively

Imbalance

If this chakra is blocked you can lack confidence, worry about the opinions of others and have a need to dominate them. You can be oversensitive to criticism, judgmental and critical of yourself, suffer low self esteem and weak will power or an addictive personality.

It can lead to an unhealthy dependence in approval from others and an assumption that everyone else is better and more worthy of reward than you are. It can also lead to depression, a tendency to boredom, sarcasm, impatience and phobias.

Physically it can cover digestive problems, flatulence, constipation, stomach ulcers, weight held in the stomach area, eating disorders, diabetes, chronic fatigue and allergies or hyper sensitivity.

The Heart Chakra (4th)

Anahata = unbeaten, a sound made without striking

Also known as the heart centre or 'that which is even new'

Located in the centre of the chest at the heart area.

It is associated with compassion, love and spirituality. When this chakra is out of balance you feel indecisive, paranoid, fear betrayal or generally feel sorry for yourself. Physically it can lead to heart disease, asthma, high blood pressure, lung disease and cancers. It can also cover problems with the arms, hands and fingers.

Colour: Green, pink

Crystals: green - aventurine, malachite, jade, peridot, emerald,

Pink - rose quartz, kunzite, morganite, rhodochrosite, unakite

- Gland: thymus
- Sense: touch
- Colour: green or pink
- Intake: vegetables
- Element: air
- Oils: bergamot, rose, neroli

- Symbol: 12 petal green lotus flower containing two intersecting triangles in a green circle
- Feminine - Yin

Areas of effect

The heart chakra is associated with compassion, love and spirituality, healthy relationships, self acceptance, the heart, the respiratory system and the immune system.

Balance

When it is in balance you have your own sense of internal balance, a healthy connection to other people and to relationships. You can balance between material and spiritual needs. You are compassionate and are able to give love unconditionally, you are able to nurture yourself as well as others

Imbalance

When this chakra is out of balance you feel indecisive, paranoid, fear betrayal or generally feel sorry for yourself. It can manifest in shyness, isolation, bitterness, a tendency to be over possessive or jealous.

It can manifest in a fear of loneliness but also a fear of commitment, a habit of demanding attention and can sometimes be seen as the 'martyr' or 'poor me' syndrome.

It is also the chakra when old traumas are stored. Old pains, losses or fears can cause problems with this chakra and this can lead to an inability to set healthy boundaries.

This loneliness, grief or depression can lead to physical decline, a general illness and an inability of the immune system to function properly.

Physically it can lead to heart disease, tension, asthma, high blood pressure, circulatory problems, breast problems, lung disease, breathing problems and cancers. It can also cover problems with the arms, hands and fingers.

The Throat Chakra (5th)

Visuddha = pure

Also known as the communication chakra and the 'purist of the pure'.

Located just below the collar bone in the throat area of the neck.

It is associated with self-expression, voice, communication and the expression of creativity through speech and writing. If it is out of balance you can feel that you want to hold back, an inability to express emotions, blocked creativity or perfectionism. Physically it can cover colds, sore throats, hearing and thyroid problems and tinnitus.

Crystals: lapis lazuli, sodalite, aquamarine, blue lace agate, sapphire, turquoise, chrysocolla, turquoise

- Gland: thyroid / parathyroid
- Sense: sound
- Colour blue
- Intake: fruit
- Element: ether
- Oils: chamomile, angelica, thyme
- Symbol: 16 blue petal lotus flower containing a downward pointing triangle surrounding a circle representing the moon
- Masculine - Yang

Areas of effect

The throat chakra is associated with self-expression, communication, voice and the expression of creativity through speech and writing.

It is related to the thyroid, the parathyroid, the jaw, vocal cords, ears, neck, mouth, nose lungs and breathing as well as the imagination and dreams.

Balance

When the throat chakra is balanced you are a good communicator and, equally important, a good listener. You can express ideas and dreams, have good imagination. You are able to trust your intuition, are contented and have vitality

Imbalance

If it is out of balance you can feel that you want to hold back, an inability to express emotions or to listen to others. It can manifest in either a fear of speaking or excessive talking, blocked creativity or perfectionism. It can manifest in stiff necked attitudes, arrogance, being dogmatic and unreliable

It can also show itself in a tendency to live too much in the imagination or a dream world. You need to be able to link the fantasy of this chakra to the reality and creativity of the sacral and solar plexus chakras in order to get things done, otherwise there is a danger of too many ideas and dreams and no action. This is a great example of the importance of a balanced chakra system

Physically it can cover colds, stiff necks, sore throats, infections, hearing and thyroid problems and tinnitus.

A Beginners Guide

The Third Eye Chakra (6th)

Ajna = command

Also known as the brow or intuitive chakra

Located between and just above the eyes.

It is associated with intuition, psychic ability, energies of the spirit and the elimination of selfish attitudes. If it is out of balance you may feel afraid of success, non-assertive or the opposite, egotistical. Physically it can lead to headaches, nightmares, eye problems and poor vision or neurological disturbances.

Crystals: amethyst, sugilite, charoite, fluorite, lepidolite, iolite

- Gland: pituitary
- Sense: light, sixth sense
- Colour: indigo
- Intake air
- Element: mind and light
- Oils: rosemary, hyacinth, basil, Marjoram, clary sage
- Symbol: a white circle containing a downward pointing triangle and held by two large lotus petals – one to each side
- Feminine - Yin

Areas of effect

The third eye chakra is associated with intuition, psychic ability, wisdom, energies of the spirit and the elimination of selfish attitudes. The eyes, base of the skull, sinus, mental and emotional balance.

Balance

When is it in balance you have imagination, clear vision, you are able to interpret experiences accurately. You are highly intuitive, have a good memory, emotional balance and mental organisation.

Psychic abilities are available when the third eye chakra is properly balanced and it can enable the talents of artists, healers and therapists to blossom.

A balanced third eye chakra gives you the power to override your logical, intellectual responses to a situation and follow your instincts, thereby allowing your 'true self' to shine.

Imbalance

If it is out of balance you may feel afraid of success, non-assertive or the opposite, egotistical. It can manifest in nightmares, hallucinations, inability to concentrate and poor memory or learning difficulties.

You rationalise everything too much, wanting logical reasons and explanations rather than being able to accept the wonder of the world.

Physically it can lead to headaches, eye problems, glaucoma and poor vision or neurological disturbances.

The Crown Chakra (7th)

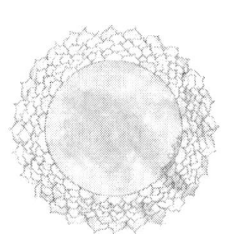

Sahasrara = thousand

Known as the 'thousand petalled lotus'.

Located at the crown, just beyond the top of the skull.

This chakra is associated with enlightenment, spirituality, energy and wisdom. If this chakra is blocked there may be a constant sense of frustration, confusion, depression, obsession, no spark of joy. Physically it can cover a sensitivity to pollutants, epilepsy or chronic exhaustion.

Crystals: clear quartz, diamond, selenite, danburite, amethyst, tanzanite

- Gland: pineal
- Sense: experience
- Colour: clear, violet or gold
- Intake: fasting
- Element: thought and cosmic energy
- Oils: frankinsense, lavender, cedarwood, rose, myrrh
- Symbol: thousand petal white lotus flower
- Masculine - Yang

Areas of effect

This chakra is associated with enlightenment, spirituality, energy and wisdom. The only true way to understand this chakra is to experience it.

Physically it is associated with the upper skull, the brain and the skin.

Balance

When it is balanced it brings knowledge, a connection to the spiritual, a magnetic personality, a sense of belonging, energy, and ability to be at peace with yourself, accepting limitations but at the same time, knowing that all things are possible. This chakra is important for psychic development and psychic protection. It allows you bliss, joy and vitality.

Imbalance

If this chakra is blocked there may be a constant sense of frustration, confusion, obsession, no spark of joy, a searching for spirituality, scepticism or over materialism limiting the growth of spirituality.

It can manifest in a constant struggle for more worldly success, which is only matched by a growing dissatisfaction with the trappings of such success. It can lead to a tendency to be a workaholic, to an inability to enjoy life, and the possibility of valuing yourself only in terms of your position, with the resulting danger to your sense of self-worth if you lose that position. Loneliness and very often a health breakdown because of overwork are also dangers.

Physically it can manifest in sensitivity to pollutants, epilepsy or chronic exhaustion, depression or Alzheimer's, migraines or addictions to alcohol or chemicals as well as chronic ill health due to over work.

Other chakras

Although we tend to concentrate on the seven major chakras, there are other chakras throughout the body and each of these has their own importance.

These chakras, normally called minor chakras, are points at which fewer energy flows intersect - and they are found in other areas of the body, for instance, the palm of the hand, the sole of the foot, in front of the ear and behind the eye, above each breast and at the back of the knee.

I find that most of them are best balanced with subtle energy, during meditation, with aromatherapy or dowsing or during a reiki healing session.

The Minor Chakras

It is generally accepted that there are 21 minor chakras:

One on the sole of each foot
One behind each knee
One for each gonad
Two for the spleen
One for the stomach
One near the liver
One for the palm of each hand
One for each breast
One for each side of the clavicle

One for each eye
One for each temple
One for the thymus gland (centre of the chest)

The foot chakras

The chakras in the sole of the foot can help keep you grounded. They can work in connection with the base chakra to help give you a firm foundation and link you to the energy of the Earth. Healthy foot chakras can help you feel secure and confident, literally keeping you stable in life.

One of the best ways of balancing the foot chakras is to take off your shoes and socks and walk on natural ground such as the grass or a sandy beach, not concrete or a paved surface.

The colour of these chakras is a rich warm brown, so crystals such as Tigers Eye or smoky quartz are good crystals to choose to help balance them.

The knee chakras

These are in the hollow of each knee joint and they are associated with the fears that we can carry in life, such as the fear of death, fear of change and a fear of losing control.

Balancing these chakras can help improve our emotional and mental stability in the same way as strong knees help our physical stability, and it can help us move forward in life. They can also help us be more flexible in our attitude and more capable of accepting, even embracing change.

The gonad chakras

Each gonad or ovary has a minor chakra and they balance the level of fertility and our emotional attitude towards sexuality.

Balancing these chakras can help give a healthier more open attitude to sexuality allowing us to accept loving relationships. It can also help improve fertility.

The spleen chakra

The two minor chakras of the spleen balance the toxins entering and leaving the body. Having them in balance can improve the digestive system and stop us storing toxins that can cause illness and damage to the body.

It also helps remove toxins that can poison our relationship with the world, making us more relaxed in dealing with other people and difficult situations.

The stomach chakra

This chakra relates to the large intestine and balancing it can help remove toxins that have settled in the intestine rather than having been eliminated if the digestive system has been sluggish. It can help us feel lighter, emotionally as well as physically.

The liver chakra

The liver is the largest organ in the body, after the skin (an organ which many people neglect). The liver has an absolutely central role in the removal of toxins from the body as well as being involved in the creation of chemicals that help balance other parts of the endocrine system,.

Liver damage is an increasing problem in our modern world, when more people are damaging their bodies with toxins, especially alcohol and drugs. Having this chakra in balance can help create a more balanced attitude to life in general.

The hand chakras

The chakras in the palm of the hands help you give or receive energy.

It is traditionally considered that the left hand receives or senses energy and the right-hand transmits, but personally I find that I can receive and transmit energy from both hands, so just follow whatever feels comfortable for you.

Healers work with their hand chakras to channel energy as they are working.

The hand chakras are connected to the heart chakra and it is not only healing energy that can flow through healthy hand chakras but the energy of creativity, the ability to create what you want and need in life, as well as the ability to be artistically creative is connected to healthy hand chakras.

A good way of balancing your hand chakras is to shake your hands and arms vigorously, and then let them hang by your side feeling the tingling as energy flows through to your fingertips.

Alternatively, hold your hands together, palms facing, fingers pointing skywards as in the traditional prayer position. Slowly move your hands apart, imagining a ball of white energy forming in the cupped space between the palms. Hold this energy and feel it cleanse and energise your hand chakras.

The hand chakras are clear or white. If you feel you need to distinguish them, the dominant palm is white, and the non-dominant is clear, which for most people means the right is white. You can work with crystals such as clear quartz, danburite and clear topaz for the clear crystals and howlite, selenite and magnesite for the white crystals.

The breast chakras

These chakras are located just above each breast/chest area. They are linked to a sense of responsibility and good nutrition. When balanced they create balance between the two, helping us have a sense of responsibility when it comes to nurturing on all levels.

The clavicle chakras

These chakras are just below the throat chakra and slightly to each side. They are associated with the throat and windpipe and can affect bronchitis or problems of the oesophagus

The eye chakras

These chakras are just behind each eye and are closely linked to the third eye chakra.

They can affect how we see the world and how we will react to it, balancing between the tendency to be withdrawn or to only see things from our own perspective.

The temple chakras

Just at the top of the cheekbones in front of each ear, these chakras can help relax tension and allow us to face difficult situations, especially if we have to face them in public. They are also related the hearing problems, tinnitus, balance problems and ear infections.

The thymus chakra

This chakra is linked to the heart chakra, but the thymus gland is a vital part of our general immune system.

It produces the t-cells that form our immune system and it also prevents the growth of abnormal cells in the body, so it is vital for a healthy system, as well as a feeling of security from being well defended

The transpersonal chakras

There are also energies outside out personal bodies, often referred to as the transpersonal chakras

The 4th Eye Chakra

This is just above the 3rd eye and controls body temperature. It also controls the balance of male/female energies. Use amethyst, lepidolite or charoite to balance this chakra

The 5th Eye Chakra

Found at the top of the forehead. When in balance, this chakra allows you to be master of your own destiny. Use selenite, diamond, clear quartz or danburite.

The Earth Star Chakra

This chakra is beneath your feet and links you to the energy of the Earth. It relates to your feet, ankles, knees, legs, hips and your root chakra, and working on this chakra will mean that you are in tune with the Earth and nature. The colour of this chakra is black, and hematite or obsidian are good crystals to choose.

The Soul Star Chakra

This is located about six inches above your head, in a direct line from your crown chakra and is sometimes referred to as the 8th Chakra. It leads to other non-physical chakras that are opened and used in advanced meditation and astral travel.

It is very important – in fact, vital - to have good balance and cleansing in the physical chakras before you work with the upper chakras.

Use clear quartz, danburite, angelite or celestite.

Hormones and the 7 Major Chakras

The seven major chakras correspond to the endocrine system and therefore the production of hormones, and understanding the role that each of these endocrine glands has in keeping our body healthy and in balance, can help you understand what each chakra can have the affects that it does on our energy system.

What exactly are Hormones?

We tend to talk vaguely about hormones – especially the female hormones - without really understanding what they are and how they affect the whole system.

Hormones are produced in glands throughout the body. They are chemical messengers that travel through the bloodstream and enter tissues where they regulate everything from growth and emotions, reproduction and metabolism, general health and well-being.

An imbalance of insulin leads to diabetes, an imbalance of oestrogen can lead to weight gain or hot flushes, and recent studies are confirming that an excess of testosterone can be responsible for increased violence in some men.

Hormones are powerful. It takes only a tiny amount to cause huge changes in cells or even your whole body, changing your life. That is why too much or too little of a certain hormone can be serious. Laboratory tests can measure the hormone levels in your blood, urine or saliva, and your doctor can arrange for these tests if you have symptoms of a hormone disorder. Home pregnancy tests are similar - they test for pregnancy hormones in your urine.

So in short, balanced hormones are vital to a balanced system.

Each of the seven major chakras has an influence on different glandular systems. So keeping your chakra system balanced automatically has a balancing affect on your hormone system.

The root chakra - Ovaries/testes

These are the glands that produce the hormones that control such things as body hair and depth of voice as well as reproduction.

The ovaries (female) produce Progesterone and Oestrogen (a mainly female hormone). They are important for the health of the reproductive tissues, breasts, skin and brain. Too much can lead to fluid retention, weight gain, migraines and more seriously - over stimulation of breasts, ovaries and uterus, which can lead to cancer.

Too little can lead to hot flushes, vaginal dryness, rapid skin ageing and excessive bone loss. It has also been linked to dementia.

Excess oestrogen in relation to testosterone in men, is thought to lead to prostate problems.

The testes (male) produce the male sex hormones, mainly testosterone, which has an effect on the growth of muscle mass and strength, increased bone density, growth and strength. It is also the hormone that deepens the voice and affects the growth of the beard.

The sacral chakra –Adrenal glands

The **adrenal glands** are small triangular shaped organs located on top of the kidneys, and are responsible for releasing a number of hormones into the body as well as sex steroids such as oestrogen and testosterone.

They secrete hormones that regulate the metabolism of fats, proteins and carbohydrates and control the balance of salt in body fluids. They also secrete adrenaline – the fight or flight hormone.

They are made up of two parts, the **adrenal medulla** which is the primary source of adrenaline in the body, the fight or flight hormone, - this raises blood pressure, increases the heart rate, and acts as a neurotransmitter (a chemical messenger in the nervous system) when the body is subject to stress or danger.

The outer part of the gland is known as the **adrenal cortex** and this secretes many different hormones into the bloodstream that deal with the body's use of fats, proteins, and carbohydrates.

The cortex also produces the male sex hormone, testosterone, and small amounts of oestrogen. Aldosterone, a hormone involved in regulation of blood pressure and water and salts in the body, is also secreted by the adrenal cortex.

The solar plexus chakra – Pancreas

The pancreas is an organ located behind the lower part of the stomach. It produces insulin which regulates the blood sugar levels and enzymes that help the body digest and use food.

Insulin helps the body take glucose from carbohydrates in food and turn it into energy that the cells in the body can use.

Diabetes is a disease of the pancreas. It develops when the body does not make enough insulin or can't use the insulin it does produce properly. Both problems mean that the level of glucose in the blood increases, causing damage throughout the body.

In type 1 diabetes the pancreas doesn't make insulin at all and you have to take insulin daily.

Type 2 diabetes usually begins with a condition called insulin resistance, where the insulin that is produced can't be used effectively by the body, eventually the actual production of insulin declines as the pancreas becomes more stressed.

The Solar plexus chakra also has an effect on the adrenals which produce Cortisol – which is essential to a healthy immune system – the body's defence against bacterial or viral infection and inflammation. Too much of this hormone can suppress the action of the immune system.

The heart chakra – thymus

This specialised gland produces the hormones that stimulate growth in early life, by the early teens it begins to shrink and be replaced by fatty tissue.

The thymus also stimulates the production of lymphocytes - T-cells - which form part of the blood's white cell defence system, and as such are critical cells of the immune system.

As we age, the thymus continues to function as an endocrine gland, important in stimulating the immune system.

The decline in the function of the thymus has been linked to loss of immune function in the elderly, which can lead to being more susceptible to infection and illness such as cancer, making it even more important to protect and strengthen the immune system as we age.

The throat chakra – thyroid

The Thyroid produces thyroxin which regulates the body's metabolic rate. Another gland, the parathyroid, controls calcium levels in the bloodstream.

The thyroid is one of the largest endocrine glands in the body. It is in the neck, below the Adam's apple. It controls how quickly the body uses energy, makes proteins, and controls how sensitive the body should be to other hormones.

If you suffer from an overactive thyroid, producing too much hormone, it is called hyperthyroidism, and symptoms can include: weight loss; rapid heartbeat; tremor; excessive sweating; heat intolerance; anxiety; muscle weakness; Goitre; irregular periods.

If the gland is underactive, called hypothyroidism, symptoms can include: Exhaustion; sleep problems; difficulty concentrating or remembering; weight gain; dry hair, skin and nails; depression or anxiety; constipation; poor libido; breathlessness and swelling of feet; hoarseness; cold intolerance; face swelling and puffy eyes; heavy periods.

The Parathyroid glands are small glands located in the neck behind the thyroid – although they are in the same area of the body as the thyroid they are not related in any way.

Their only purpose is to regulate the calcium level in the body within a very narrow range, so that the nervous and muscular systems can function properly. They constantly measure the amount of calcium. If levels drop slightly they produce a hormone (PTH) that withdraws some from the storage in the bones and puts it into the blood. When the calcium levels are correct, hormone production stops.

Calcium balance is vital to our well being, not just to avoid osteoporosis and kidney stones. If calcium levels get too high, the electrical system that controls our nervous system stops working properly. It can affect the personality, cause headaches, loss of energy and concentration. It can cause insomnia, irritability and many other nervous-system symptoms including depression.

A healthy parathyroid it is mainly about feeling normal and being able to enjoy life.

The third eye chakra – Pituitary

This small gland is only about the size of a pea but it is vital to our well being. It sits just beneath the base of the brain, behind the bridge of the nose.

It takes messages from the brain, via the hypothalamus and uses them to produce hormones that affect many parts of the body, including stimulating all the other hormone-producing glands to produce their own hormones.

This means that it is often referred to as the 'master gland'. It influences the metabolism, growth and the general body chemistry

The pituitary hormones help control some of the following body processes: Growth; blood pressure; some aspects of pregnancy and childbirth including contractions during childbirth; breast milk production; sex organ functions in both men and women; thyroid gland function; the metabolism (converting food into energy); water regulation, including controlling the absorption of water into the kidneys and temperature regulation.

The crown chakra – Pineal

This is a tiny gland deep within the brain. It produces melatonin which affects the pituitary, thyroid, adrenals, ovaries and testes. As the production of melatonin is stimulated by darkness and inhibited by light, it is released into the body at night and regulates the body clock.

René Descartes, (1596- 1650), the French philosopher, mathematician and physicist, who dedicated much time to the study of the pineal gland called it the "seat of the soul, and the place in which all our thoughts are formed."

A lot of research is being done on the affects of melatonin. It is considered one of the most effective anti-oxidants and is the only compound known which can diffuse into the body cells and savage free-radicals, very important for long term health.

Crystal healing and the Chakra System

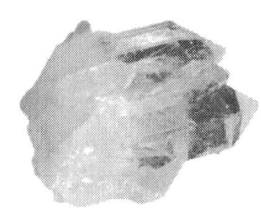

Healing crystals are a wonderful way to help balance and maintain the energy of your chakra system.

Each chakra radiates to a specific colour, which means that you can work with a crystal of the right colour energy when you are balancing the chakra system, either as a crystal layout or as a general, daily balancing method.

Crystals are an easy way to work regularly on the chakras, either by carrying a piece in your pocket, keeping a larger piece close to you as you work, or by wearing them as jewellery and keeping them close to you as ornaments.

The origins of jewellery are linked to the chakra centres as the gemstones were used as amulets and talismans and general jewellery developed from that use.

The types of jewellery that we use link to the different chakras - Crowns and headbands, earrings, chains of different lengths lying at the throat, heart and solar plexus chakra. Bracelets and belts can work on the lower chakras. Our ancestors were comfortable with the energy of crystals and gemstones, and they developed ways of keeping this energy close to them.

As well as working with the general chakra colours, working with crystals allows you to be more specific in your healing choice, picking a crystal from the colour spectrum that can help with a specific area of energy. For instance, any blue crystal can be used for balancing the throat chakra, but you can choose lapis lazuli or sodalite if you want to strengthen your immune system or lower blood pressure. You might choose kyanite if the area of concern is an emotional blockage in the throat chakra, feeling unable to get your ideas across or a feeling that those around you don't listen to you.

This book is not intended to be a complete guide to Crystal healing - that is a fascinating subject requires an entire book – or indeed books to itself - it is just intended to guide you in choosing the right crystal for each chakra..

The Root Chakra is at the base of the spine and is balanced by dark crystals, normally red or black, but you can also work with smoky quartz which is brown.

Some suggestions for you to choose from are:

Smoky Quartz – strengthens willpower and can help ease tension and back pain. Also very good for those who suffer from chronic stress, as it can change your tendency to become stressed.

Black Tourmaline - very grounding and protective energy, strong psychic protection especially against psychic attack

Red Tigers Eye -strengthens self expression and builds confidence

Ruby - strong survival energy, a warrior stone helps you see problems as challenges to overcome. Very good for anyone who suffers from a chronic illness in that it can help strengthen your base energy.

Red Garnet - strong survival energy, a warrior stone, helps you see problems as challenges. Can help strengthen the blood

Hematite - strengthens the blood, helps you absorb iron from food, good for anaemia, helps give energy in stressful situations.

Black Onyx -very grounding and protects from the influence of others, can help improve concentration

Obsidian – very protective against negative energy from other people such as work colleagues and neighbours or members of the family, so it can help in very stressful situations. Can help improve blood circulation to the extremities -good for those who suffer from cold hands and feet.

The Sacral Chakra is positioned just below the navel and is balanced by the orange shade of crystals.

Some suggestions for you to choose from are:

Carnelian - the Joy Stone, very good for the connective tissues and can help ease muscle pain and arthritis, can help ease asthma and allergies. Helpful when recovering from wounds.

Orange calcite - protects against stress, can ease IBS (irritable bowel syndrome), calming energy

Aragonite - strengthens the bones, stabilising energy, helps metabolise calcium

Amber - protective especially against radiation of the Sun. Allows the body to heal itself.

The Solar Plexus Chakra is just below the breastbone and is balanced by the yellow shade of crystals.

Some suggestions for you to choose from are:

Citrine - positive energy can help with exhaustion, also said to attract abundance

Yellow Sapphire - very calming

Yellow Jasper - protective against negative energies, especially popular for healers

Gold Tiger's Eye - gives confidence and builds self-esteem

Yellow Calcite - increases energy, stimulates the digestive system

The Heart Chakra is in the centre of the chest and is balanced by the green and pink shades of crystal.

Some suggestions for you to choose from are:

Green:

Aventurine - the brain stone, can help clear up muddled thoughts, can help improve your metabolism

Malachite - this crystal contains a lot of copper and helps ease pain, especially inflammation pain such as arthritis. Protects against toxins

Jade - the gem of health, wealth and long life. Can help remove toxins from your system

Peridot - a gentle healer. Helps heal liver, pancreas, glandular system and metabolism

Emerald - kindness and peace can enhance love and unity between partners,

Pink:

Rose Quartz - the Love Stone, calming energy can strengthen self-confidence and self-esteem and improve blood circulation

Kunzite - mood lifting, ease depression, heal the heart. Good for new beginnings

Morganite - soothing, good for stress illnesses, very relaxing. Helpful for recovery from surgery.

Rhodochrosite - eases stress, encourages positive attitude and enthusiasm for life.

Unakite - a mixture of green and pink. This is a very balancing crystal energy

The Throat Chakra is just above the collar bone and is balanced by the blue shades of crystal.

Some suggestions for you to choose from are:

Lapis Lazuli -the gem of integrity and truth, balance the immune system, ease fevers and control temperature, hot flushes, menopause.

Sodalite - logic and communication, protect glandular system, protect against infection and helps temperature control

Blue Lace Agate –calming, eases stress, the thyroid ear and throat problems. Good for people who use their voice professionally

Blue Sapphire- brings order to the mind, encourages the desire for knowledge and wisdom.

Turquoise – protective, tissue regeneration, protect against environmental pollution

Celestite - lift heavy moods, quiets the mind, wonderful for working with angelic energies

Kyanite - opens emotional blockage, allows you to get your ideas across, helpful when you feel that those around you don't listen to you.

The Third Eye Chakra is between and just above the eyes and is balanced by the indigo shades of crystal.

Some suggestions for you to choose from are:

Amethyst – wonderful for psychic protection and times of psychic growth

Sugilite - a powerful spiritual healer

Lepidolite – can help with neuralgia and nerve pain, can also help with ideas

Iolite - the Stone of peace and truth

Charoite - can help bring peaceful sleep and creative dreams

Purple Fluorite - helps you absorb information, especially when reading – good for study.

Labradorite - inspirational energy, very good for sparking new ideas

The Crown Chakra is just above the top of the skull and is balanced by clear & violet shades of crystal.

Some suggestions for you to choose from are:

Quartz Crystal – known as the master healer, the only crystal that can be programmed to deal with a specific problem

Diamond - pure energy

Herkimer Diamond – excellent for helping with storing and locking in energy

Danburite – connects you to angelic energy

Selenite - cellular healing

Amethyst – wonderful for psychic protection

Charoite – can help bring peaceful sleep, creative dreams

Sugilite – a powerful spiritual healer

As you work with crystals, you will find the different energies that you are drawn to personally, and you will create your own preferred set of crystals for chakra healing. Some may be set in jewellery, some may be tumbled stones and others unpolished, natural pieces of the crystal.

What matters, is that you feel drawn to them, comfortable with the energy of each crystal. You may also find that you want to work with different crystals at different times. Again, there is nothing wrong with this. The different energies of the individual crystals, combined with their colour can make a powerful healing combination for the chakra system.

Cleansing your crystals

A new crystal should always be cleansed before you use it for healing. This is not actually to clean dirt from it, but the unwanted energy it will have gathered from other people.

You should also cleanse your crystals between specific healing sessions to avoid transferring negative energies, this is especially important when you are working with healing crystals to balance the chakras. You should also cleanse them as a general habit when you feel that they are less affective or on a regular basis. Learn to trust your instincts. You will learn to feel when they need cleansing and recharging, it's as if the battery is running low.

There are many ways suggested for cleansing but care should be taken before you decide on which method to use. Some crystals would be destroyed by water, while others would fade in sunlight - amethyst, rose quartz and aventurine can all be badly affected by too much sunlight.

Personally I prefer to avoid some of the methods that are sometimes recommended.

Placing a crystal in salt water or sitting it directly in salt can be very damaging for some crystals. A salt solution can penetrate some crystal structures, making the stone cloudy or discolouring it. Sitting some crystals in salt would destroy them altogether. For instance, placing an Opal on a bed of salt would draw the water from it, changing it from an Opal gemstone into a much less valuable piece of chalcedony.

I also prefer to avoid burying a crystal. Apart from the obvious danger of not being able to find it again, there is the risk that the soil conditions will damage the crystal. For instance, your soil may be too acid for the gemstone.

In crystal healing, we are working with the energies of crystals and we should respect them and take care of the crystals we have chosen so that they will continue to work with us for many years.

An Amethyst bed or druze is a very useful crystal for helping to cleanse other crystals. This is a piece of amethyst with the natural points growing from the base rock.

Simply place your other crystals, gently onto the surface of the natural points and allow the Amethyst to focus the negative energy away from them. Leave them for approximately 3 to 4 hours. This method is gentle enough for any of your crystals, even those set into jewellery, although you do need to take care that soft gems will not be scratched by the amethyst, which is a hard crystal (7 on the Mohs scale). For instance, fluorite is 4 and apatite is 5 on the Mohs scale.

Do not leave the crystals on the amethyst too long, as it is a very energising gemstone and other crystals can begin to take on the energy of the amethyst. If you do leave them too long, set your crystals aside to allow them to recover their own energy.

You can also use sea salt to cleanse the negative energy from your crystals. You can find sea salt at most supermarkets.

Place the dry sea salt into a clear glass bowl. It is important to use clear glass as you do not want to introduce colour energy into the cleansing.

Sit a smaller clear glass bowl in the sea salt so that it is surrounded by the salt.

Place your crystals into the second bowl so that they are surrounded by but not touching the salt. Leave them for three to four hours.

You can reuse the salt for many months for cleansing, just cover it so that it doesn't get too dusty but never use it for cooking once you have been cleansing crystals, you don't want to ingest the negative energy.

If you're comfortable with dowsing with a pendulum you can cleanse your crystals in this way as well. Just ask your pendulum to remove the negative energy from your crystals and then hold it over the crystals and let it move as it wants until it comes naturally to a halt. This will make sense if you are an experienced dowser - if you've never worked with a pendulum - it'll make no sense at all!

You should cleanse your crystals when you 'feel' that they need it, there are no timetables for this. A crystal that absorbs negative energy - for instance snowflake obsidian or quartz crystal kept beside a TV - will require quite frequent cleansing. So will a crystal that you are using to absorb pain, such as malachite, which for severe pain should be cleansed daily. But you may feel that other crystals only need cleansing after a number of months, in fact, a citrine pendant worn every day, may only need cleansing every six months.

Use your intuition - you can tell when your crystal is no longer as effective as it was. Until you get the 'feel' for them, a good guideline is about once a month.

Programming clear quartz.

Clear quartz is the only crystal that you can program for a specific person or healing task.

Cleanse the crystal first of all so that it doesn't carry any negative energy.

Then focus for healing intention into the crystal. You can do this in any way that you are comfortable with. Concentrate on the healing that you want the crystal to do, whether it's for a particular person or to heal a particular problem.

Calm yourself so that you can concentrate and ask your angels, say a prayer, meditate or cast a spell – whatever you are comfortable with.

Crystal Healing Layouts

Although you can rebalance your chakra system simply by having healing crystals close to you, you can also work with them in a more active way, by using various crystal layout patterns.

Basic Chakra layout

This is the simplest way to start your journey into balancing your chakra system with healing crystals and it is a very useful pattern, one I still use myself.

Collect your chosen crystals – one from the right colour range for each chakra. You can simply choose a crystal of the correct colour or you can choose a crystal from that colour range that will also help to deal with a specific problem that you want to address. Make sure that your crystals are cleansed of negative energy before you begin.

Allow yourself a quiet time where you will not be disturbed. Play some soothing music and light a scented candle if you like. Wear comfortable clothing so that you will not be distracted as you relax.

Lie on your back in a comfortable position and place a crystal of the appropriate colour on each Chakra centre. Start at the root chakra and move up through the system

If you wish, you can use two – green and pink, such as aventurine and rose quartz – at the heart chakra.

Once you have placed your crystals, relax and breathe deeply to calm your system and help you absorb the healing energy of the crystals

Imagine a bright white light moving across your body, re-balancing your chakra system and relaxing and recharging your energy. Relax in this way for about 15 minutes or as long as you are comfortable. Sometimes you may feel that you want to remove the crystals earlier, sometime you will feel comfortable for longer. I find that most people like to absorb the energy in this stage for about 15 to 20 minutes

When you're ready, remove the crystals from the crown down to the root chakra and relax for a further 20-30 minutes to help you absorb the healing energy.

You can repeat this pattern as often as you like, it can be a very pleasant way to relax and rebalance yourself after a stressful day at work.

Of course you can also use this pattern when you want to give a chakra healing pattern to someone else.

Do make sure that your crystals are cleansed between treatments.

The Seal of Solomon

You can also surround yourself with the Seal of Solomon pattern of quartz points as well as the chakra balancing crystals, to intensify the healing energy of the pattern

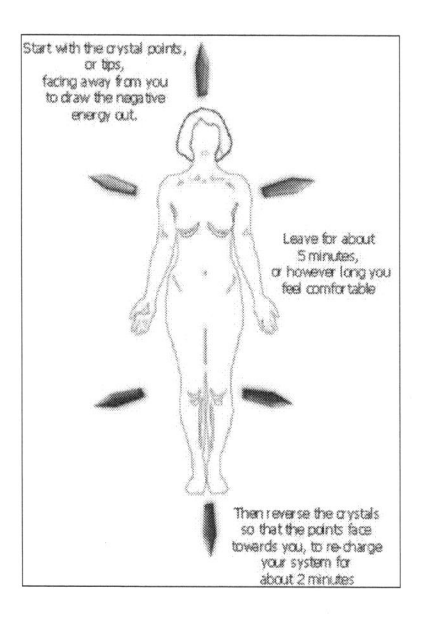

Start with the crystal points, or tips, facing away from you to draw the negative energy out.

Leave for about 5 minutes, or however long you feel comfortable

Then reverse the crystals so that the points face towards you, to re-charge your system for about 2 minutes

This is a six pointed star pattern, made of two interlocking triangles.

This placement is very useful when you need to relax, either physically or mentally. It can refresh the energy and reduce or remove stress and you can also use it alone with just the six clear quartz points, without the chakra crystals, which can be especially good for purifying your energy.

Combining it with the basic chakra healing layout, surrounding yourself with this pattern of quartz points as well as having the chakra balancing crystals laid on your chakra points, with strengthen the healing energy of the chakra layout.

When working on the whole chakra system, the Seal of Solomon can be created as a pattern around the whole body as in the diagram – with one point at the head, one between the feet, one at each side at shoulder level and another on each side at knee level. With the points facing outwards you will create a release of excess energy, with the points facing inwards the body will receive an energising or charging effect.

It is best to start with the points facing outwards for about five minutes to release stresses. Then change the direction for about two minutes to recharge your system.

Adding the seal of Solomon to your chakra layout can create quite an intense healing energy, which is why you normally work with this pattern for shorter periods of time.

The Seal of Solomon can also be used in the treatment of a specific chakra, placing the crystal points in a much tighter pattern around the crystal you have chosen for the chakra that you want to treat and placing it on that chakra.

This can be very helpful when you want to help balance a particular problem, for instance, a sore throat, a bout of IBS, stomach cramps or a headache. However, you should remember that it is best in general to treat the entire chakra system rather than focusing on special areas too much, you don't want to create imbalance by focusing energy on a specific chakra or area of the body.

Chakra realignment

If you are balancing someone else's chakra you can use a different system with four clear medium sized quartz points.

Make sure that you are grounded and calm before you start. Place three points in a triangle around the person to be healed.

First place two crystals at the feet pointing inwards and then one above the head pointing away to release any negative energies. Hold the fourth, the control crystal, in your left hand with your right hand pointing at the floor to drain any negative energies and unwind any blockages by moving the crystal in an anti-clockwise pattern over the body, starting at the feet, then knees, hips, hands and arms and then the seven major chakras finishing at the crown.

Change the crystal to your right hand and repeat the pattern, this time using a clockwise, healing movement.

Remove the crystal points in reverse order (the one at the head first) and allow time to rest. Discharge any unwanted energy by rinsing your hands and control crystal in cold water.

Other ways of using the Chakra points

You can also use a crystal on one particular chakra if you want to obtain a specific healing affect. Although you should remember that 'balance' is central to the chakra system, so avoid working on one chakra and ignoring the others.

When you wear a crystal as a pendant, the length of chain or cord will determine the chakra point that will be the most affected. A crystal at the heart will have the strongest affect on your emotional state, while at the solar plexus it will have an effect on your digestive system. Crystal earrings can be useful for the throat chakra as can a crystal pendant on a short chain. If you want to work on the root chakra, try to carry a tumbled stone in each hip pocket.

Although you can place the crystal close to the chakra you want to work on, it will also have a balancing affect just by being inside your personal energy field.

Dowsing and The Chakra System

A dowsing pendulum is a very helpful tool for working on and balancing the Chakra system, but what is dowsing?

Dowsing is a skill that is as old as human history. People have been dowsing for water supplies as long as people have needed fresh water, but dowsing is much more than that.

In recent years, we have become much more comfortable with the idea of dowsing and particularly in working with the dowsing pendulum, which is more flexible in its use than dowsing rods or a forked stick and is a particularly useful tool for healing.

Basically a dowsing pendulum is a weight on the end of a string or chain that can move in circular patterns or backwards and forwards to show you yes and no, positive and negative answers.

You can buy many beautifully fashioned dowsing pendulums in wood, metal or natural gemstones. Personally, as a crystal healer, I prefer working with the natural gemstones, but it is entirely up to you.

Programming your pendulum.

When you buy a new pendulum, the first thing you need to do is program it, so that you know, when it is telling you 'yes' or 'no', or 'don't know'.

There are various methods of doing this and if you would like more detailed information on dowsing in general you could take a look at my book, 'A beginners guide to pendulum dowsing'.

I prefer to work with the pendulum rather than forcing it into certain patterns, so the programming method that I recommend is:-

Find somewhere that you can relax and be comfortable, somewhere quiet where you won't be disturbed or distracted.

Calm your thoughts and empty your mind of negative energies. Remember, as with anything you do, negative emotions or energies will interfere with your pendulum dowsing.

Make sure that you are comfortable, don't wear clothes that restrict you, or feel too tight, too hot or too cold.

Take a deep breath and let it out slowly.

Sit comfortably, but do not cross your feet. Allow your energy field to be open.

Hold the pendulum between the thumb and forefinger of your dominant hand, letting your wrist relax. You are simply holding the pendulum securely so that it won't fall from your hold. You are not gripping it or moving it yourself.

Ask the pendulum to show you its neutral, or don't know indicator. Normally, the pendulum will hang still or will vibrate gently on the end of its chain or string, but don't force any movement. The idea is to allow the pendulum to show you what indicators it will use. You can ask the question out loud or simply in your mind, always be polite to your pendulum, you are asking it to work with you so don't simply demand that it works.

Once you are happy that you know the neutral indicator, ask the pendulum to show you its yes answer and wait for a response. The pendulum should start to move, often in a clockwise or anticlockwise pattern, but sometimes it will be left-right and backwards-forwards. Whatever the pendulum shows you is the 'yes' answer for you with that pendulum. You may find that you have different responses with different pendulums.

Ask the pendulum to return to its neutral position.

When it has come to its resting position repeat the process, asking the pendulum to show you its no answer. This will often be the opposite of your yes indicator, anti clockwise to a clockwise movement or backwards-forwards to the left-right movement.

You may find that you can program your pendulum almost immediately, or it could take a few days of work, even a couple of weeks before you are really in tune with your pendulum, so don't get despondent. As a general guide, you will get a faster response if you tend to work with energy healing such as crystal healing, Reiki, or aromatherapy.

Always go through this process with a new pendulum because you may not get the same response with every pendulum that you work with. I have different response patterns with quartz pendulums than with agate pendulums.

Once you have programmed your pendulum and know what its responses are, you can then work with it to help rebalance energy in the chakra system.

Dowsing the Chakra system

The pendulum can be used to re-balance the chakra system and to pinpoint problem areas by dowsing over each of the chakras in turn.

Obviously you can't use this direct method on yourself, it's very difficult to physically dowse at each of your chakra points!

Ask the person whose chakras you will be cleansing, to lie down comfortably. If this is not possible, you can use the same method while they are sitting comfortably with their hands by their sides.

Ask the pendulum to help you in balancing the chakras. You may be trying to ease a specific problem, such as back ache or a headache, ask the pendulum to help you in this aim.

Start at the root chakra and allow the pendulum to move as it wishes. If it stays in your neutral position, the chakra is balanced. If it moves in either your positive or negative pattern, allow the pendulum to move as it wishes, holding it over the chakra until it settles once more into the neutral position, showing that the chakra has been rebalanced then move onto the next chakra.

Continue this until you have passed over all the chakras, ending at the crown.

Once the chakras have been balanced, especially if there has been a strong blockage in one of the upper chakras, the person may feel lightheaded or slightly dizzy. This is quite normal, he or she should sit quietly for a minute or two, try to have a drink of water available.

It is important to focus on balance rather than relieving pain. It is possible to relieve pain and this is a very useful when you know there is a specific problem. But pain is an important indicator that something is wrong with the body and if you simply keep relieving that pain you could be masking an important and serious problem or illness that should be checked out by a medical practitioner.

Always cleanse your pendulum between working on chakra systems, you don't want to transfer negative energy between people or healing sessions.

There are many ways of cleansing a pendulum. If you choose a crystal pendulum - as I prefer - you can use the same method you would choose for any other crystal.

The methods I prefer are to either lay the pendulum on a bed of amethyst for three or four hours, or to place the pendulum in a small, clear glass bowl and sit this bowl in a larger clear glass bowl filled with dry sea salt, again for three or four hours. You can also cleanse your pendulum by clearing your mind and imagining a stream of pure while light washing over the pendulum or you can use smudging where you burn sage or sage and a combination of herbs, concentrating on the intention to cleanse negative energy and replace it with positive, healing energy.

Dowsing to balance your own chakras

You can also use your pendulum to cleanse your own chakras - although obviously not by dowsing directly over them unless you're very flexible – the crown chakra is particularly difficult unless you have long arms!

Clear your mind and sit or stand somewhere comfortable.

Ask the pendulum to help you in balancing your chakras.

Whichever hand you dowse with, hold the other palm over, but not touching your root chakra and hold the pendulum away to the side of your body.

As with cleansing chakras on someone else, the pendulum will either remain neutral, indicating that the chakra is in balance, or it will move. If it does start to move, allow it to move as it wishes, for as long as it wishes. Once it comes back to your neutral position you can move your palm over the next chakra.

Alternatively you can focus mentally on each Chakra as you balance it rather than holding your hand over the area.

You can use this method on a single chakra to help ease a specific pain - for instance on your throat chakra if you have a sore throat or a cold, on your sacral chakra if you have indigestion or a stomach upset, or on your third eye if you have a headache.

However, you should not get into the habit of overworking one area as this will cause imbalance in the system as a whole.

Aromatherapy and the chakra system.

Aromatherapy - the art of using plant essences for their healing energies - dates back to the earliest times.

They were used by priests and healers in the ancient civilisations of Egypt, Persia and China and continued to be used and respected until science and bottled medicines took over and we lost our way and our knowledge of ancient healing.

But in recent years we have been regaining our interest in the tried and trusted traditional ways of healing, and aromatherapy has been at the forefront of this movement, so much so that it has almost become too widespread. The term aromatherapy has been added to products from candles to bath foam, shampoo to household cleaners. All too easy to lose sight of what aromatherapy really is.

It is a method of healing using essential oils from plants, very concentrated plant extracts, which is why they are not to be used directly on the skin. They are far too powerful and must be diluted with a carrier oil or in water – although oil and water don't mix, so you cannot simply add it to a bottle of water, but you can add a few drops to a bath or foot spa or to a facial steamer.

Essential oils can be used when working with the chakra system either through massage or aromatherapy baths. You can also use the aromatherapy oils as a perfume as long as they are mixed with a carrier oil or cream, or you can use them in an oil burner for your home or work space.

Inhaling the scent is a vital part of healing when working with these beautiful, essential oils, and they can help bring balance and harmony to our systems through our chakra system. They can be used to create the right atmosphere for healing or you can place a few drops in an oil or cream to create a lotion of the essential oil that can be applied directly to the chakra area.

You can use an aromatherapy burner to add essential oils to your healing area when you're balancing the chakra system with crystals or by dowsing, or during a yoga or reiki session.

You can also choose an essential oil to add aromatherapy energies to a meditation session.

You should choose an aromatherapy oil that you are drawn to or that you have decided you need for its specific healing energy, but there are some oils that are specifically suited to each of the chakras and the following list can give you some guidance in your choice.

It is important to research the aromatherapy oils you choose before you to decide to work with them.

Some oils should be avoided if you are pregnant, such as rosemary, basil, cedarwood, fennel, juniper, marjoram, myrrh, thyme, basil, nutmeg, clary sage, sage and parsley.

Other oils should be avoided by those who suffered epilepsy, have kidney problems or high blood pressure. So it is important to research the oils you want to use, and preferably to go to a reputable supplier, who will be able to guide you in your choice.

When you are working with aromatherapy oils for healing it is important to work with genuine, good quality oils rather than some of the more basic oils that are sold for burners and are simply for scenting your home.

The root chakra.

Cedarwood – antiseptic, fungicidal, stimulates circulation, good for fungal infections.

Myrrh - athletes foot, thrush, haemorrhoids

Patchouli - soothing, aphrodisiac, eases anxiety, athletes foot, eczema.

Lavender - antidepressant, relieves stress, good for muscle aches and pains.

Benzoin – arthritis, gout, poor circulation

Frankincense - relaxing, aids sleep, excellent for meditation.

The sacral chakra.

Jasmine - labour pains, uterine problems, sprains, nervous exhaustion, apathy and stress

Rose - aphrodisiac, good for menstrual disorders, anxiety, stress.

Sandalwood - fluid retention, cystitis, good against viruses.

Ginger - diarrhoea, flatulence, indigestion. Cramp.

Ylang ylang - lifts depression, soothe fears and anxieties.

Cardamom - cramp, dyspepsia, flatulence, indigestion.

Orange -antidepressant, constipation, obesity, water retention.

The solar plexus chakra.

Vetiver - deeply relaxing, eases depression, nervous tension, arthritis, aches and pains.

Geranium - relaxing and refreshing, good for menopause, PMT, good for balancing hormones.

Cinnamon - digestive, menstrual problems, poor circulation, sluggish digestion.

Lemon grass -poor circulation, muscle pain, indigestion.

Clove - Arthritis, rheumatism, nausea, dyspepsia.

Peppermint - flatulence, nausea, fever, muscle pain, colic, cramp.

Juniper - diuretic, cleansing, calming

The heart chakra

Rose - helps anxiety, stress, depression, low self-confidence, good for mature skin.

Bergamot - skin infections, cold sores, good for anxiety and insomnia.

Ylang Ylang -lifts depression, soothes fears and anxieties, soothing to the skin.

Neroli - calming, soothes nerves, lifts depression, good for stress.

Lavender - antidepressant, relieves stress and insomnia, respiratory problems.

Geranium - relaxing and refreshing.

The throat chakra.

Angelica - fatigue, migraine, nervous tension, stress, bronchitis, coughs.

Camomile - relieves anxiety, stress, allergies, helpful for neuralgia and earache.

Thyme - headaches, insomnia, stress, colds and flu, asthma, laryngitis, sore throat.

Bergamot – insomnia, anxiety, skin infections.

Peppermint - asthma, bronchitis, sinusitis, headache, mental fatigue.

The third eye chakra

Rosemary - uplifting, decongestant, skin and hair problems, good for clearing the mind.

Basil - ear ache, sinusitis, bronchitis, antidepressant, colds, fever

Juniper - cleansing, calming, helps skin problems.

Hyacinth - refreshing for a tired mind, stress, helps develop creativity.

Marjoram - headaches, insomnia, migraine, nervous tension.

Clary Sage - antidepressant, induces a sense of well-being.

The crown chakra

Lavender - good for headaches, relieves stress, insomnia.

Frankincense - relaxing, excellent for meditation, decongestant, good for laryngitis and bronchitis.

Myrrh - asthma, bronchitis, sore throats.

Rosewood - headaches, antidepressant, tissue regeneration, stress.

Sandalwood - insomnia, good against viruses, soothes respiratory problems.

Vetiver - depression, insomnia, nervous tension, stress.

Cedarwood - nervous tension, stress, bronchitis, congestion, hair loss.

Jasmine - sensitive skin, depression, nervous exhaustion.

Rose - anxiety, stress, antidepressant, low self-confidence.

Working with essential oils.

There are many different ways of working with aromatherapy essential oils, and we tend to have developed a habit of either using them in an oil burner or using them in some pre-prepared form, such as candles or commercially available lotions and creams. But it is far more beneficial if you can choose the specific oils that you want to work with.

Always buy good quality essential oils and then store them correctly. They are sold in small, dark bottles and they should be stored in a cool place, out of the light. The essential oils are very concentrated and need to be protected from strong light. They also evaporate quickly in the air, which is why they need to be kept in small, airtight, dark glass bottles.

Essential oils are very concentrated and very powerful, which is why they are always diluted before you put them on the skin.

As they will only dissolve in fatty oils rather than water, they are added to base oils such as almond or sunflower oil or sometimes, to alcohol.

If you are making your own blend or massage oil, the dilution is approximately 1-3% aromatherapy oil in carrier oil. So if you are using 25 ml of almond oil you would add between seven and 25 drops of essential oil. As a general rule, you need a stronger mix of the essential oil if you are working on a physical ailment and a weaker solution if you are working on emotional or spiritual problems

Almond oil or sunflower oil are fine if you are making a massage oil, but you can also use rich oils such as avocado, jojoba or apricots kernel oil if you want to make a nourishing oil for the skin. You can also add a few drops of your chosen essential oil or oils to an unperfumed body lotion or face cream.

Chakra massage.

Once you have created your massage oil, body cream or lotion you can work directly on the chakra area.

First of all, put the oil or cream on your hands and breathe in deeply. The aroma of the essential oil is an important part of the healing process, but do be careful not to get the pure oils close to your mouth or eyes and of course you should never swallow them, they are extremely concentrated and can be toxic if used incorrectly.

Once you have inhaled their scent, either rub the appropriate oil mix directly into the chakra body area or rub it into your hands and massage that area, either physically on the skin or as an auric massage.

Aromatherapy bath.

We've become very used to having a large range of products available to us that are sold as aromatherapy shower creams, bath oils or body lotions, but this is not the same as creating your own prescription for a healing bath.

Aromatic bathing is one of the most effective and enjoyable ways of having an aromatherapy treatment, the Romans were certainly in favour of this type of healing.

First of all run the bath. Then add between four and eight drops of your chosen essential oils and mix to the water. Don't add them earlier as the oil doesn't dissolve in water, and much of the effect will be lost. An aromatherapy bath is a particularly good way of treating emotional, mental or spiritual imbalances in the chakra system as it is a very relaxing treatment and an excellent way of breathing in the healing scent of the oils. It is therefore a very effective way of dealing with problems such as stress, insomnia, tension, headaches and anxiety.

Aromatherapy baths can also be a particularly effective way of dealing with skin conditions and aches and pains.

If you would like to combine therapies for your chakra healing, you can also add crystals to your bath. Simply place a tumbled piece of your chosen crystal to the aromatherapy bath. For instance, if you wanted to work on a lack of self-confidence., you could add two drops of lavender, two drops of geranium and some rose quartz crystals to your bath.

Aromatherapy hair oil.

You can add a few drops of your chosen essential oil to a nourishing base oil such as jojoba or sweet almond oil if you'd like to make your own rich conditioner. Massage it into the scalp, and then wrap your hair in warm towels for a couple of hours. This will help balance either the third eye or the crown chakra, and is a wonderful way of relieving tension.

Steam inhalation.

This method of working with aromatherapy oils has long been popular in treating colds, throat and chest infections or sinus problems - problems with the throat chakra. Thyme or peppermint oil are good choices if you want to work on balancing your throat chakra in this method.

Vaporisation.

Using an oil burner or vaporiser is a wonderful way to perfume a room with essential oils. It's a perfect way to create a relaxing energy for a chakra healing session, but you can also choose this method when you want to work on a particular chakra by choosing one of the aromatherapy oils from the chakra list above for the burner. Always make sure that you place the oil burner in a safe place, as of course it does have a candle in the base of it. You can also use a light bulb ring or a small bowl of water placed on a radiator. Either of these methods will defuse the oil around the room but of course do not involve a lighted candle

Colour healing and the chakras

As we have seen, the different colours of the rainbow are relevant to each of the different chakras, so it's easy to see how we can work with colour healing therapy to balance the chakra system.

Like many of the therapies that we are rediscovering, colour therapy has very ancient roots. It dates back to ancient Egypt and the civilisations of India and China, and coloured light flowing through stained glass windows in a church can have a powerful effect.

It's well known that colours affect us. How we feel, our moods and our emotional state, either positive or negative. Colour can also have a profound effect us physically. Sitting in a red room will make you feel warmer than sitting in a blue room, even though both are exactly the same temperature, simply because of the colour.

The effects of colour are reflected in language - feeling blue, in the pink, red rage, green with envy. Colours can have good and bad effects on us and can be used with this in mind whether you are decorating a room, choosing a new outfit or working with colour for healing.

You can work with colours for therapy in a number of ways.

Crystal healing itself is a method of working with colours for balancing the chakras, either placing the right coloured crystal on each chakra, or wearing jewellery featuring a crystal of the chosen colour.

You can also infuse the colour into water and create an elixir. Make a collection of different coloured glass bottles, one for each chakra colour that you want to work with.

Fill the bottle with pure spring water and let it stand in the sunshine for about three hours. Pour the water into a glass and take small sips from it throughout the day. An elixir can be quite powerful, so don't take a full glass of colour elixir until you understand how it will affect you.

You can also use visualisation of colour during meditation to help balance your chakra system.

Of course you can also wear the colour that you want to work with, either in your everyday clothes, or during a healing session you can place a silk scarf of the chosen colour over a specific chakra. You can also wrap the entire body in a rainbow of silk scarves to balance the entire chakra system.

Recently, it has become easier to find methods of producing coloured light either using a coloured screen over a light source or by working with coloured light bulbs and mood lamps.

The root chakra vibrates to the colour red. Red light is very stimulating it can help increase the energy of the blood, pushing fire through the energy system. In healing, red is considered to be good for improving the circulation, helping balance chronic illness, strengthening the kidneys, the blood and the skeletal system.

The sacral chakra vibrates to the colour orange. Orange represents joy, warmth, creativity and happiness. It is also the colour of sensuality, sexuality and pleasure. It is considered to help ease depression, strengthening the immune system and relax cramps in the body.

The solar plexus chakra vibrates to the colour yellow. In healing yellow represents mental activity and the intellect. It is the energy of the sun and can help strengthen concentration and self-confidence. It is also considered to help to ease problems with the digestive system, and the liver.

The heart chakra vibrates to two colours, green and pink, but in colour healing it is normally green that is used. Green is a very calm, soothing and cooling energy, it is also considered to be very cleansing and detoxifying and is used to help deal with imbalance in the body. It is considered to be helpful for those living with diabetes, bronchial problems, gout, cysts and tumours. It is also used to help deal with painful joints.

The throat chakra vibrates to the colour blue. Blue is a very calming energy helping bring deep inner peace. In healing it is considered to be a very cooling energy for both the body and mind, helping you to be calm and peaceful in expressing your opinions. It is also considered to help create restful sleep, lower blood pressure and reduce fevers.

The third eye chakra vibrates to the colour indigo. Indigo has long been considered a Royal colour, associated with deep spirituality and higher consciousness. You can find this rich colour in temples and churches across the world. It can have a very sedative effect and can help open your inner vision and spirituality but it can also be depressing if overdone.

The Crown chakra vibrates to the colour violet and to clear light. Violet is a very calming energy, the colour of transformation. This can help create a state of deep relaxation, stimulating intuition, dreams, inspiration and allowing emotional release. Clear white light contains all the colours of the spectrum and therefore affects everything on all levels. It represents release, illumination, purity and innocence.

Healing from within

Most of the methods of balancing that we have looked at are, in some way, external. But you can also work on balancing and healing your chakra system from within, by choosing foods and herbal teas that balance and complement the chakra system.

When you are working with food to heal your energy system, it is important that you choose foods that are healthy, not only from a physical point of view but food that has healthy energy as well. This means choosing foods that have been grown or reared with respect, given time to develop the goodness and balanced life force that they should have. Fruit and vegetables that are forced and produced with chemicals and fertilisers to speed their growth, haven't had the time that they need to produce the sugars and nutrients that they should have. Some crops are harvested early and then shipped around the globe to reach the supermarkets before they are ripe and ready to be picked.

Fruit and vegetables use the energy of the sun to grow and produce the vitamins that we need, they also draw the minerals we require from the earth that they grow in, drawing the goodness from the rocks beneath us and they need the proper amount of time to gather this goodness.

It's also important to ensure that the meat and fish you are eating has been reared properly and with respect, that the animals have been fed with good quality food themselves.

If you are going to work with food for energy healing, you should try and choose good quality organic and preferably locally produced food, so that you are ingesting the best energy that you can for your healing.

You can also work with herbal teas – properly called herbal infusions – taking the healing properties of herbal medicine in the easy to use form of a refreshing drink rather than in our modern tablet form.

As with all other forms of healing, it's best to work on your entire chakra system rather than focusing on one area. Although you can concentrate on a single chakra to heal a specific problem , you should always remember that it is as system and we are a whole system rather than a collections of parts. And when working with food for chakra healing, your diet would be awfully boring if you just concentrated on one area!

The root chakra vibrates to red, so red food is a good choice for balancing this chakra - red apples, pomegranates, red peppers, tomatoes. You can also work with mushrooms, root vegetables and animal protein if you are not vegan

– a vegetarian of course can use eggs and dairy products

Dandelion tea is a very good choice for balancing the root chakra. It is a detoxifying tea and considered to be very good as a diuretic and has a long history as a healing herb. It can be helpful for those living with diabetes or high blood pressure.

Sage tea also has a connection to the root chakra. It has one of the longest histories of all medicinal herbs and was used by Greek physicians to help with many ailments. It is considered to be helpful for liver and kidney problems amongst many other properties.

The sacral chakra vibrates to orange – so you can work with oranges themselves, but also orange peppers, carrots, butternut squash, apricots and pumpkin. You can also work with healthy oils and fats and oily fish.

Spearmint, calendula and camomile herbal teas can be balancing for the sacral chakras. Spearmint is well known for its digestive properties and is also very refreshing and reviving.

Camomile is one of the most popular herbal infusions, and for good reason. It have been called a 'cure all' The Egyptians used to treat fevers, the Greeks and Romans recommended it for headaches, kidney, liver and bladder problems and it has been used for its healing energies ever since.

Calendula has also been used as a herbal medicine for thousands of years and is considered to help with gastrointestinal problems as well as being rich in vitamins and minerals, especially beta-carotene.

The solar plexus chakra vibrates to the colour yellow – so choose yellow foods such as sweet corn, yellow peppers, melon, yellow lentils and grapefruit. Complex carbohydrates are also good for the solar plexus chakra, such as whole grains, fruit and vegetables.

Fennel tea has long been used to help with problems with heartburn and high blood pressure. It is also a mild appetite suppressant and is considered to help the kidneys, spleen and liver. **You should not take fennel when pregnant.**

A tea of marshmallow root can help calm the tension in the solar plexus chakra if you are feeling stressed and camomile tea also has a very calming effect, helping you sleep if you are suffering the insomnia caused by tension. Camomile has also been used to help with digestive problems.

The heart chakra vibrates to the colour green – so eat your greens! Kale, leafy greens and broccoli are particularly good, as are raw foods that still have all their chlorophyll.

Lemon balm, hawthorn and rose hip teas are a good choice for the heart chakra. Lemon balm can help aid digestion and soothe the stomach but it is also a very calming, soothing energy. Rose hip is an extremely rich source of Vitamin C which makes it excellent for boosting the immune system.

As a herbal medicine, Hawthorn is widely regarded in Europe as a safe and effective treatment for the early stages of heart disease, it can help with the circulatory system, angina, high blood pressure, it is even considered to help with congestive heart failure and cardiac arrhythmia.

The throat chakra vibrates to blue which means that many of the berries are good choices – blueberries, blackberries, grapes and prunes, but also beetroot, red cabbage and aubergine. Many of these fruits and vegetables are very high in compounds that can help protect the body from certain infections and bacteria.

Echinacea, elderberry and marshmallow herbal teas can help balance the throat chakra. Echinacea can help stimulate the defence system and is widely regarded as 'the' remedy for colds and flu. It is seen by herbalists as a treatment rather than a preventative, and you should take it to ease the symptoms rather than drinking it regularly.

Elderberry is another herbal remedy for coughs, colds, sore throats and tonsillitis. It is also considered helpful for the respiratory system and to boost the immune system.

Marshmallow is a very calming herbal tea and can also help heal inflammation in the respiratory system.

The third eye chakra vibrates to the colour indigo, so more of the blackberries and blueberries along with red onion, dark chocolate and red wine!

Nettle, lemon balm and eyebright herbal teas can help balance the third eye chakra.

Nettle is a detoxifying herb which has diuretic properties, which can make it helpful for high blood pressure.

Lemon Balm has long been used for treating insomnia, it is considered to have sedative properties. It is a very calming herb which can help relieve stress.

Eyebright (euphrasia) has been used since the 14th century to treat all types of eye problems and it is also used as an anti-inflammatory to help with upper respiratory tract infections as well as hay fever and sinusitis.

The crown chakra vibrates to the colour violet but as the most spiritual chakra is it not considered to need the nourishment of food. In fact 'fasting' is considered to be the food of the crown chakra.

Although there are no foods associated with the crown chakra, there are still herbal teas that can be used in your balancing and healing.

Camomile tea is regularly used to help treat fevers, headaches and strengthening the immune system. It is also a very calming tea, a good choice when you feel tense or anxious or have trouble sleeping.

Lavender is also a very calming and relaxing herbal tea and can be used to treat headaches, insomnia and depression

Peppermint has been used for its healing properties for thousands of years, since the time of the ancient Egyptians. Peppermint tea is very refreshing and can also help with breathing problems and coughs. It can also help to ease headaches.

Working with the chakra system.

There is a big difference between understanding what the chakra system is and understanding what effect it can have on us in everyday life.

Understanding the subtle energies, kundalini rising, the three principal intersecting energy channels of Ida, Pingala and Sushumna, is fascinating and wonderful, but at the end of the day, unless we are healers and Reiki masters, most of us simply want to know what the chakra system means to our lives.

At its simplest, imbalance in the chakra system means illness unhappiness dissatisfaction, exhaustion and depression. Balance means good health, energy, a positive outlook, creativity and happiness.

So what does each individual chakra mean to us in our general, everyday lives, and how can it improve our physical health, mental and emotional wellbeing and spiritual growth when we have the chakra in balance.

The root chakra

As always we start from the root chakra and move up through the system to the Crown chakra.

The root chakra is literally our roots. Every strong system needs strong roots. A healthy tree has deep roots that anchor it firmly into the earth giving it strength and sustenance, allowing it to draw the water and nutrients it needs for a long, strong and healthy life.

We also need strong roots to anchor us, giving us a strong and stable base from which to grow. A well-balanced root chakra gives us that stability.

Many people focus on the more glamorous upper chakras, the chakras of spiritual growth, seeming to consider the lower chakras, including the root chakra, as somehow less virtuous, less spiritual, less interesting.

But unless we have strong foundations and a healthy connection to the earth and the physical world, we will become unstable, scattered and unable to focus.

The root chakra is connected with good basic health. It is associated with physical security and safety, it is our foundation and as such we should never ignore it, not that we should ignore any chakra. They are a system and they work as a whole.

The root chakra influences your physical energy, your basic health, your survival instinct and your vitality. Physically it affects the bones of the feet and legs, the spinal column, the sciatic nerve and the large intestine.

It influences your career and your money mindset, your ability to attract money or your tendency to have problems with money.

If your root chakra is weak, whether it's closed or spinning too fast, it can feel as if life is constantly a struggle. This can mean that you have problems with your general health. You have problems trusting people. You have financial problems, constantly worry about money and not having enough, you might be stuck in an unfulfilling and unrewarding career.

Fear about security and survival can be paralysing and can stop you being able to see beyond the problems and therefore stop you being able to do anything about solving the problems. You get trapped in a negative downward spiral and of course the negative energy is very draining.

Traditionally, it is considered that the root chakra develops in the very early stages of life, up to the age of about seven. This means it is affected by our relationship to our parents and our very early surroundings. A young child depends on the parents and carers, and any insecurity or fear during those early years can become ingrained, which is why some very successful people still feel insecure financially.

Fear is corrosive and very difficult to get rid of, especially if it is ingrained in early life. It can lead to a victim mentality, the sense that you are not in control of your life and what happens to you, that are dependent on others and cannot take control of your own life or the situations that you find yourself in, always expecting disappointments and loss.

It can also mean that you have problems in following a dream, because there is always a little voice inside telling you that you will never achieve the dream, so it's easier not to try it. Problems with the root chakra can also lead to weight problems, body image problems and general problems with food.

Physically, if your root chakra is out of balance you may be prone to having problems with the feet and legs or your bones, you may suffer problems such as osteoarthritis. A weak root chakra can also lead to problems with chronic health such as extreme fatigue and low energy. Those who suffer from ME/chronic fatigue syndrome or fibromyalgia often have imbalance in their root chakra.

This shows how important - how vitally important - a healthy root chakra is to our entire well-being. The root chakra should never be neglected in favour of the more glamorous, upper spiritual and psychic chakras.

A healthy root chakra will allow you to succeed. It means that you will expect to succeed and be happy. A well-balanced root chakra will give you the stability and grounding that is required in life. It can help you have strong connections to your family or friends.

A balanced root chakra will mean that you have a positive outlook on life. The glass will always be half full, rather than half empty, you will feel secure, and you will radiate that feeling of security to other people so that you will come across as more confident and they will react more positively to you. You will be creating a positive upward spiral. A balanced root chakra means that you feel at home with yourself and your past. You have trust that things will work out well.

Someone with a balanced root chakra enjoys their career and is good at it and is rewarded for being good. It means that you don't worry about money, you're good at saving it, as well as making it and you don't feel guilty about spending it.

The kundalini, the mythical serpent that sleeps coiled at the base of the spine represents the life force that rises up through the chakra system, changing your energy field, and therefore your life on all levels. Balancing the root chakra allows the kundalini to awaken and release its energy through your system.

It's often said that the body is a temple, balancing the root chakra will ensure that your temple has a strong foundation.

The sacral chakra

Once our survival needs have been taken care of we can move on to learning how to enjoy life, learning how to accept and give pleasure without any guilt, moving from fulfilling what is necessary for basic existence into the areas of life that makes life worth living.

The sacral chakra is referred to as our dwelling place, and represents the sacredness and sweetness of our dwelling place.

The basic health and strong foundations of the root chakra are absolutely vital to live, but the ability to enjoy life is what turns basic survival into living.

There is a terrible and very depressing saying that has become quite popular in recent years. 'Life's tough then you die'

It's such an extremely negative view on life that is seen as a joke. But having that attitude will create its own downward spiral of negativity. You will look for things to go wrong, you will expect to be disappointed, to be let down and to be miserable.

The sacral chakra affects our attitudes to success and pleasure. It affects our relationships, our sexuality, our attitude to desire and passion.

Physically, it has an effect on the fluid systems of the body, fertility, the reproductive system the kidneys and bladder.

When the sacral chakra is closed or spinning too fast you can have serious problems with your attitude to pleasure, either closing yourself away from it entirely in a very puritanical way, seeing pleasure as a sin or, at the other extreme, chasing pleasure for pleasure's sake. Either of these attitudes is very unhealthy, and can lead to serious emotional and physical problems such as emotional immaturity, a tendency to feel very jealous, or the other extreme very guilty.

Physically an unbalanced sacral chakra can lead to kidney problems and uterine and prostate problems, a tendency to IBS, pain in the middle or lower back and problems with fertility or impotence.

In the West we have developed a very unhealthy attitude to pleasure, seeing it as sinful, expecting to suffer in life, only succeeding through hard work and sacrifice. This attitude is the sign of an unbalanced sacral chakra.

Women in particular, can develop a martyr complex, being expected to put everyone else before themselves, whether that is children, her partner or even work colleagues. A woman who puts herself first is seen as selfish, even unnatural, but everyone needs to be able to look after themselves and to enjoy life.

The sacral chakra is particularly associated with our attitude to sexuality. When the sacral chakra is unbalanced we tend to have a very unhealthy attitude to sexuality and passion. Sex can often be associated in the mind with guilt, sin or pain and of course this is not going to lead to pleasurable sexual encounters or a rich fulfilling sex life with a loving partner.

The other extreme is to be chasing pleasure simply for the sake of pleasure, being a pleasure junkie but never actually achieving happiness on any deeper levels. This can be in our attitude to sex, becoming involved in short term or dysfunctional relationships, but it can also affect other areas of chasing pleasure, constantly looking for new ways and new things that will make us happy but that never do.

It can mean constantly filling your life up with new stuff. The next new thing that you have to have but that that loses its attraction as soon as you get it - the new car, a new handbag, a new job, a new partner. This is a very exhausting and very negative way to live, and you will radiate negativity, drawing the type of people to you who will confirm your belief that life cannot get better, that you simply are not a lucky person. No matter what you do, you won't win the lottery of life.

A balanced sacral chakra allows you to interact with the rest of the world in a healthy and positive way.

When you have a positive attitude to pleasure and giving pleasure, you will radiate that attitude. You will be an enjoyable person to be around, which means that people will want to be around you.

Someone with a balanced sacral chakra tends to see the good rather than the bad, the positive rather than the negative. If they did a swot analysis (Strength Opportunity Weakness Threat) on their lives, they would see the strengths and opportunities rather than the weaknesses and threats. When confronted with a problem they see it as a challenge and focus on the opportunities rather than just seeing it as a brick wall.

A balanced sacral chakra allows you to have a passionate, pleasurable and fulfilling sex life but it's more than that. It allows you to be open and honest in your relationship, it allows you to respect your partner and to enjoy emotional stability as well as a healthy relationship to pleasure and intimacy.

Someone with a balanced sacral chakra is able to enjoy life in general. When things are difficult they are able to look forward to when they will improve. They know that winter will turn into spring, they have the ability to enjoy the small things in life rather than always looking for the big payoff. People are more likely to spend time with them because they're a pleasure to be around.

The solar plexus chakra.

The third or solar plexus chakra is quite often called the personal power chakra. It is ruled by the element 'fire' and is the point at which the energies of the root and sacral chakra move up into the more personal level of our energy system.

The solar plexus chakra is about self-will, ambition, your relationship with yourself. It's a very balancing chakra, balancing the energies of self without being selfish, learning to respect others while at the same time respecting yourself. The solar plexus chakra is about you as an individual, it gives strength and vitality to the energy field.

Physically, the solar plexus chakra affects the stomach and digestive system, the gall bladder, liver and spleen and the pancreas, the organs that deal with digestion, detoxification and the regulation of sugar in the blood stream. This is a very active part of the body. It is the engine room of our system, processing the fuel from the food that we put into our system and turning it into the forms of energy that the body can actually use.

The stomach breaks down the food, digesting it into forms that can be used. The gall bladder neutralises the stomach acids. The liver detoxifies the system. The spleen controls the production of white blood cells, and the pancreas produces the insulin that controls the level of sugar in the blood.

There are expressions that we use in everyday speech that are linked to this part of the body such as to 'vent your spleen', 'a gut reaction' or 'I can't stomach this'. These expressions are actually a good description of the effect that blockages in the chakra solar plexus can have on us.

A blocked solar plexus chakra can lead to a lack of confidence and over sensitivity to criticism. It can show itself as an addictive personality or weak willpower. You can feel that other people have power over you. In fact, you can give away your power, feeling that this is the only way to keep the peace in a relationship. You can develop too much dependence on others to create your sense of self worth. In the worst cases, this can mean that you are drawn to relationships that involve bullying and often violent or abusive partners. Even in friendships or with colleagues at work, these traits of a blocked solar plexus chakra can still be seen - dependence on others for approval and recognition of worth, rather than having a sense of self-worth.

Physically, a blocked solar plexus chakra can lead to digestive problems, excess acid, stomach ulcers, diabetes or allergies.

It may seem easier in the short term to back away from conflict and confrontation, but in the long run it is the most difficult path to take and will only lead to a continual chipping away of your self-confidence. It will also lead to you building up a volcano of anger inside, which will lead to physical illness.

Someone with a balanced solar plexus chakra will have a strong sense of identity and acceptance of others without feeling the need to dominate or to be dominated. You will have spontaneity and a positive willpower. Far from being jealous, you will admire others who have power and influence, who have self-confidence and a strong willpower. A balanced solar plexus chakra allows you to listen to your instincts, it allows you to develop your psychic abilities, learning how to listen to your gut reaction or hunches.

Strong self-confidence and self-esteem allows you to follow your dreams and your instincts, enabling you to be successful in your career and personal life.

A balanced solar plexus chakra allows you to speak your mind without fear, accepting yourself as you are and allowing you to follow your own path, making decisions that you believe in, rather than those that you think somebody else will approve of.

The heart chakra.

This is the central chakra, the heart of the system. Obviously, the heart chakra influences matters of the heart - relationships, love and romance and compassion. It also affects spirituality and self acceptance. Physically, it affects the heart, blood pressure, the lungs and respiratory system and the upper back and arms.

Modern Western life seems to cause a great deal of trouble for the heart chakra. Heart disease is a serious problem, it's a major cause of death, and there are also millions of people who suffer from heart disease, high blood pressure, poor circulation and respiratory problems - chronic health problems that cause a great deal of pain and restrict the ability to live life to the fullest.

At its most basic, the heart is a biological pump whose job it is to circulate oxygen rich blood around the body. It carries everything that is needed to all parts of the body, and then removes all the toxins through the kidneys and liver and lungs. Once we look at it this way, it's easy to see how vital a healthy heart is to our entire system.

But in our pursuit of success, instant gratification, excitement and material abundance, we have forgotten how to cherish the things that truly matter. We often see those who follow their heart rather than their head as being dreamers, and we mean it to be an insult rather than praise. But some of our greatest minds have been dreamers. Albert Einstein said "imagination is more important than knowledge. For knowledge is limited to all we now know and understand, while imagination embraces the entire world, and all there ever will be to know and understand."

Even the medical profession is beginning to realise that there is a link between our emotional and mental health and physical health. High blood pressure and heart diseases are often a physical sign of someone who is stressed, who is constantly angry or frustrated, and who is bottling up a great deal of emotional pain.

Every life will have disappointments, losses, problems and challenges, but when the heart chakra is balanced all of these events can be dealt with and processed with positive energy, allowing you a sense of balance and acceptance, and an ability to look beyond the immediate problems.

The heart chakra is the central point of the chakra system, balancing the lower physical chakras with the upper spiritual chakras. When it is in balance it allows you to create balance throughout your entire system.

Creating a life/ work balance, creating balance in relationships, rather than being too demanding or too self pitying, creating balance between physical and emotional needs, allowing you to see opportunities for growth and development, balancing material and spiritual parts of your life.

A blocked heart chakra can cause paranoia and fear of betrayal, indecisiveness, shyness, bitterness and jealousy.

Someone with a blocked heart chakra can find it very difficult to experience true love, instead travelling through a series of short, intense relationships, constantly looking for love, but constantly finding pain and emotional instability. This can be seen in friendships as well as romantic relationships, a constant series of being let down, disappointed or abandoned and this can lead to a spiral downwards, finding yourself unable to trust and unable to believe in yourself, beginning to ask - 'Why can't I find love?' 'What is wrong with me?'

The fear of being let down can lead you to shun intimacy altogether, choosing to ignore the emotion because of the fear of betrayal, and a sense of jealousy or possessiveness will destroy any chance of real happiness.

A balanced heart chakra will allow you to love yourself. It will bring a sense of internal balance that will improve your self-confidence and your self-esteem, allowing you to have a healthy connection to others and to create successful relationships based on mutual respect, trust and compassion.

The ability to balance the material and spiritual parts of our world is vital to happiness and good health.

A balanced heart chakra and the ability to follow your heart is not a block to success, far from it, it leads to being more relaxed with yourself and with others. Rather than having doubt and insecurity at your core, you have a great sense of security and safety, which allows you to be open compassionate, forgiving and to radiate positive energy.

A balanced heart chakra will allow you to love yourself, which is the very beginning of being able to love anyone else. You'll be able to appreciate yourself and then the feelings of others.

Pleasure, creativity, enjoyment and love are not a waste of time. They are the things that make life worthwhile. When you put them at the core of your being everything else will fall into place.

The throat chakra.

The throat chakra is just above the collarbone in the hollow of your throat. It is associated with communication, creativity and self expression. Spiritually, it affects our sense of security and independence.

It is seen as a link between the heart chakra, and the upper spiritual chakras, allowing the consciousness to rise from the physical to the more spiritual energies.

In our modern lives, constant communication has become an epidemic. It's as if we spend all our time chatting, tweeting, blogging, facebooking and texting but we never actually communicate with each other.

Communication is a two-way street. It's about listening as well as talking, expressing thoughtful ideas, rather than just meaningless noise.

The throat chakra affects our self-expression, creativity, our voice, speech and writing. Physically, it affects the throat, the vocal cords, the ears, mouth, teeth and nose.

When the throat chakra is closed or spinning too fast you will have an inability to express your ideas and emotions or to listen to others. You will have a desire to hold yourself back, the feeling that you will not be 'heard' by others and a tendency to feel that nobody will care about your opinions, or that you have nothing worth saying in the first place.

Someone with a blocked throat chakra can sometimes speak very quietly, almost as if they are afraid to voice their thoughts. They are often considered the quiet one in a group and may even have a very dull or monotonous voice, or a very quiet, childlike voice.

A blocked throat chakra will often lead you to agreeing with somebody else's ideas even if you actually disagree quite strongly. This will lead to anger and resentment that in turn leads to physical problems. In fact, you can feel the pain and tightness in your throat if you are bottling up your true feelings and stopping yourself from expressing your true opinions.

Problems with the throat chakra often go back to childhood. You might have grown up with the attitude that children should be seen and not heard. A child who was constantly being told to shut up, will grow up to be an adult who feels they cannot speak out. If you learn that your opinions are worthless, that you are less important than the phone call your mother is taking, or that you told you are stupid and ignorant in school, then you will learn never to take the risk of being belittled, embarrassed or worse still, ignored and you'll be incapable of being open and expressing your true feelings.

A blocked throat chakra can also manifests itself at the other extreme of communication, someone who is always too loud, always making jokes, always laughing and being unrealistically positive in a vain attempt to cover the true belief that nobody will ever listen to them.

Physically, a blocked throat chakra will have an effect on the throat area. It will affect the thyroid and the parathyroid, the ears and mouth as well as the throat. It can lead to problems with regular colds, asthma, sinusitis, sore throats, throat and ear infections, tinnitus and hearing problems, neck pain, headaches and exhaustion.

The thyroid and the parathyroid of extremely important glands for our system, and they are affected by the throat chakra. They are involved in the repair of body cells, the levels of calcium and phosphate in the blood and can affect your weight, your muscle strength, your ability to sleep, levels of anxiety and stress, temperature control and many other things, which makes the throat chakra extremely important.

When the throat chakra is balanced, you will be able to express your ideas, emotions and dreams. You will trust your intuition and have a good imagination. You will be a good communicator, which involves listening as well as talking - we often forget that listening is the true secret of good communication. You have to be able to hear what the other person is really saying, sometimes that means seeing behind the actual words.

We often start a conversation with 'how are you doing?' 'How are you today?' And most of us will accept the answer, 'I'm fine', without ever hearing the real truth hidden behind those words, 'I'm not fine at all.' A good communicator will hear the truth and will be willing to listen, allowing the other person to unburden themselves and heal.

The fact that you are able to express your thoughts and emotions means that you are more content, more relaxed and happy in your relationships with other people because you are not holding yourself back, or feeling yourself inhibited and repressed by other people's views.

A balanced throat chakra is also vitally important to be able to use your voice in any professional arena, such as public speaking, teaching, broadcasting or singing. And good communication skills are important to anyone who writes or works as a therapist where you need to be able to communicate your ideas, as well as being able to listen to others.

When you have a balanced chakra you will be able to project your ideas through your voice, having the confidence to believe in your own opinions and the ability to value your own ideas.

Rather than being arrogant, dogmatic or loud, you will be calm, with a speaking voice that others enjoy listening to, you will be able to express yourself with clarity and will be the person who is invited to talk to a group or give a speech – and you won't mind doing it!

The Third Eye Chakra

The third eye or sixth chakra is positioned between and just above the eyes. It is sometimes referred to as the brow chakra or the eye of Shiva, and it is connected to our ability 'to know' or 'to see'.

It affects our intuition, our psychic ability, the energies of the spirit, wisdom and emotional intelligence. Physically it affects the eyes, the base of the skull, sinuses, mental and emotional balance.

Physically, we use our eyes to see the world around us, but the third eye chakra allows us to see that which isn't visible. It allows us to access our intuition and to make judgements based on our inner vision. We often call this ability, a hunch, much like the gut reaction of the solar plexus chakra.

The third eye chakra links the physical and spiritual energies, but in modern life, many people have chosen to neglect or ignore the spiritual side of life and their psychic abilities, only believing in what is physical, what can be touched, only accepting things for which we have concrete evidence. We often allow the intellect to dominate our thought processes, overriding intuition and inspiration, and our modern world has entrenched this view of what is right. We have developed into a world where scientists are the ones we believe in, where rationalism and logic are valued above instinct, where intellect is more important than intuition.

But true leaps in knowledge come from the imagination, the daydreams, the 'what ifs?' Albert Einstein is considered one of the greatest thinkers the world has seen and he freely admitted that many of his discoveries were sparked by his imagination.

There is a saying, the brain is like an umbrella - it works best when it is open.

When the third eye chakra is blocked it can lead to a fear of success and a tendency to be non-assertive or at the opposite extreme, egotistical. It can manifest in nightmares, hallucinations, poor memory or an inability to concentrate.

There can be two extremes in a person with a blocked third eye chakra. You can either be extremely logical, arrogant, dogmatic in your ideas and authoritarian in your attitudes to others, sticking rigidly to your own set of rules until you limit your own lifestyle and become isolated as others fall away from you.

At the other extreme, you can feel lost and unable to make even basic decisions, never trusting your own judgement. You can become indecisive and unable to commit to anything because you lack confidence in your decisions, and therefore set your expectations of life very low, almost fearing success, believing you cannot possibly achieve it.

It can mean that you are constantly looking to someone else to give you guidance in life, whether that is experts in some field, gurus or mentors, or more spiritual experts such as astrologers or psychics.

Physically an unbalanced third eye chakra can cause headaches or migraine, neurological problems, poor vision or problems with the eyes such as glaucoma. It can also lead to problems with insomnia, or if you do sleep, poor quality sleep and frequent nightmares.

Unfortunately for all of us, many people seem to have a blocked third eye chakra, and many of them seem to be in charge of our lives. Our modern lifestyle values logic and the ability to be rational. Being focused on your point of view and being able to drive it through without being influenced by those who disagree with you is seen as strength. But these traits are also dogmatic. People like this are unable or unwilling to see someone else's point of view, there is no discussion, just a demand that you follow their decision. In personal life that can be very difficult to live with, in business it can make life unbearable for those around the dictator, and where the person is in charge of decisions that affect hundreds, thousands or even millions of people, it can be very unpleasant indeed.

Again, there is another extreme to having a blocked third eye chakra and that is being unable to think logically at all. Being caught up in fantasy and imagination can make it impossible to function at any successful level in the real world. This kind of person may have all sorts of plans and dreams but never actually do anything about achieving them. This type of person has no faith in their own judgement and will allow themselves to be led by anyone, without being able to discriminate between good and bad advice. They may be constantly searching for guidance or a spiritual experience, endlessly seeking the truth from someone else.

A balanced third eye chakra allows you to balance both of these sides of your brain.

It allows you to link logic with intuition, it allows you to use imagination in your decision-making, it allows you to accept inspiration, operate on hunches and listen to your inner voices.

When the third eye chakra is balanced, you have the confidence to follow your dreams but the logic to be able to do so sensibly. You enjoy clear vision and an ability to interpret experiences. You are highly intuitive and are able to trust your instincts. This means that you are able to make accurate, but intuitive decisions about your career, lifestyle and family, you are able to trust your instincts when dealing with other people, not allowing your logic to override your intuition.

There are many times when you have an instant, irrational reaction to meeting a new person or entering a new situation and we often tend to allow logic to override that instinctive reaction. But how many times have you looked back and wished you followed your initial instinct - whether good or bad!

When the third eye chakra is balanced, you have the confidence to follow that instinct, trusting that your inner voices are sending you a clear message, and you are able to override the logic that tells you that you should allow time to look into the situation and make a rational decision.

When you have a balanced third eye chakra, you will have a good memory, you will be mentally organised and open to learning and accepting new knowledge. You will have a clear sense of direction and a clear vision of what you want to do in life, although you will still be able to react instinctively to opportunities as they arise.

People with a balanced, third eye chakra are often sought out by others for advice and guidance. In fact, they will often become therapists and healers.

The Crown chakra.

The Crown chakra is situated just above the top of the skull and is the chakra of pure consciousness. It is seen as the most spiritual chakra, the ultimate goal of the chakra system, the door to enlightenment fulfilment, spirituality and self-realisation. Indeed, the door to the divine.

Some people see it as the main reason for their chakra journey, the most important chakra, the gateway to enlightenment. But it is important to remember that we are a whole, that our entire chakra system is important to well-being, physically and mentally, emotionally and spiritually, and that the greatest sense of being at one with the world, of being truly, spiritually aware can happen for someone who remains securely grounded.

The Crown chakra affects our spirituality, our spiritual energy and wisdom, mental clarity, and the ability to accept enlightenment. Those with a balanced Crown chakra, and balanced chakra system can have a magnetic personality.

Physically, the Crown chakra affects the brain, the skull and the skin.

When the Crown chakra is unbalanced, it can lead to a constant sense of frustration and confusion. There can be problems with obsession and materialism. It can lead to a total focus on the material world, without any allowance for any spirituality. Everything depends on material success. So someone with a blocked Crown chakra can be constantly suffering from exhaustion, constantly chasing success, they can be workaholics focused totally on material goals.

This may often lead them to outward success, but at the same time, an inward sense of emptiness. Everything has to be explained in terms of logic and proof, but in the end, it can lead to an emptiness, an inability to enjoy their success and dissatisfaction with life in general. It can even lead to depression, confusion and a tendency to obsession.

Physically, somebody with an unbalanced Crown chakra can suffer severe headaches and migraines. They can suffer from epilepsy, Alzheimer's or chronic exhaustion. The tension caused by bottling up anger and emotions, and from obsessive tendencies can lead to problems with high blood pressure. There can be a great sense of frustration and a feeling of failure when you can't gain or maintain the success you feeling is required for happiness.

When the material success that is sought fails in some way because of illness, redundancy, retirement or a change in life circumstances, someone with a blocked Crown chakra will find it very difficult to adapt. In fact it may be a time of crisis that makes them fall apart, unable to find any meaning in their world and unable to make any new decisions.

When the Crown chakra is in balance, you are able to see your place in the world. You are able to let go of ego, and except the mysterious nature of the universe that we inhabit. Rather than having to know everything. You are happy to know that you don't know everything, that you live in a world of infinite possibilities.

Someone with a balanced Crown chakra is able to accept change and embrace the unexpected, even if at first, the changes in life can seem uncomfortable. The person with a balanced Crown chakra is able to see the opportunities, is able to let go of material requirements and find peace in the spiritual world. This person will attract others to themselves because they radiate peace and openness, spirituality and an acceptance of joy.

When the Crown chakra is in balance, you are able to live in the now accepting what life brings, able to make the most of what the universe provides for us.

And into the future

The chakra journey is never ending.

It is a path that we can follow for our entire lives, fine tuning, learning, adapting and growing. Constantly understanding something new about ourselves and learning how to improve our chakra balance and our lives.

In any form of healing it is important to be open to new knowledge and new experiences, always growing and adapting to circumstances and learning to enjoy the journey.

As soon as you think you know everything you have closed your mind to the wonders that the world can show – No one can know everything, that would be so boring!

So I hope this book can help start you on your journey to a lifetime of learning to understand your chakras and bring them ever closer to the goal of perfect balance.

About the Author

From a long line of healers on the West Coast of Ireland, Brenda has worked with energy healing, the chakra system, a dowsing pendulum and healing crystals for over 15 years and is a member of the British Society of Dowsers.

She regularly gives talks and classes on dowsing, vibrational therapies, crystal healing and colour healing as well as writing books, articles and well known series of Core Information charts on a number of alternative therapies.

you can contact her at:
brenda@healing-earth.co.uk
website: www.healing earth.co.uk

Printed in Great Britain
by Amazon.co.uk, Ltd.,
Marston Gate.